REACH
A
HOW GOD TOOK A KID FROM THE STREETS
TO REACH A GENERATION.
GENERATION

REACH
A

HOW GOD TOOK A KID FROM THE STREETS TO REACH A GENERATION.

GENERATION

MY LIFE STORY & JOURNEY OF REACHING
CHILDREN WITH THE GOSPEL OF JESUS CHRIST

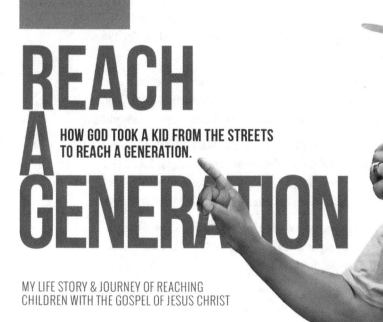

LUIS R. REYES

FOUNDER & SENIOR PASTOR
CHURCH OF JOY / REACH A GENERATION

**CREATION
HOUSE**

 LUISREYESMINISTRIES.COM

Reach a Generation by Luis R. Reyes
Published by Creation House
A Charisma Media Company
600 Rinehart Road
Lake Mary, Florida 32746
www.charismamedia.com

Cover design by Jordan Jones

Visit the author's websites:
www.thenewchurchofjoy.com
www.luisreyesministries.com
www.reachageneration.com

Library of Congress Control Number: 2016962415
International Standard Book Number: 978-1-62999-201-3
E-book International Standard Book Number: 978-1-62999-202-0

While the author has made every effort to provide accurate telephone numbers and Internet addresses at the time of publication, neither the publisher nor the author assumes any responsibility for errors or for changes that occur after publication.

First edition
17 18 19 20 21 — 987654321

Printed in the United States of America

APPRECIATION TO MY FAMILY

THE AMAZING WORK God has birthed through my life and the impact I have made in thousands of lives could not have happened without the support of my family.

To have a heart that is turned to the younger generation, my heart must first be turned to the Lord, to my wife, and to my children.

Matthew, the day I got the news we were having a boy overwhelmed me and assured me that our name would be carried on to the next generation. You came later in my life and at the perfect time. You have changed my life and have taught me how to love your mother. You and your sister have slowed me down to enjoy the little things in life. I'm so proud to be your father, not for what you can do, but for who you are as a person. I truly believe you will be a greater man than I ever will have been because you were raised differently than I was. My heart will forever be turned towards you so your heart will be turned to your heavenly Father.

Madison, you saved my life! You came early in our lives, and we had to raise you in a time that was so difficult and challenging as we were building the ministry. When I wanted to quit and give it all up, you stood there as a three year old looking up to me, and that forever changed me. I knew then that I did not want my daughter to grow up never knowing her dad or never fulfilling her destiny because I didn't. I wish your mom and I could take all the credit for what you've become today; however, Maddie, God blessed us with a daughter that is amazingly loving, willfully obedient, and steadfastly resilient. You amaze me every day, and I am truly proud of the choices you've made; I am honored that you have chosen to live for God and surrender your life to this younger generation through your ministry. I could have put any child on the cover of this book; however, I chose to put you on the cover with me. As I reached thousands of children, the world needs to know that I was able to reach my own daughter, and you now have the heart to reach a generation!

Tricia, tears come to my eyes when I think of the role you've played in my life. You have always been my biggest cheerleader, cheering me on whatever the task was. You have been the greatest counselor, outside of the Holy Spirit, that has listened to every dream and vision God gave me and every heartache I felt in the trenches of ministry. You have been a strong partner working alongside of me when all hell broke loose against us. You have never given up or spoken a negative word towards the ministry or what God called us to do. I am grateful for every role you've been to me and to our ministry. I am most grateful to you for being a wonderful mother to our children. Thank you, Tricia, for making sure our children were taken care of when I had to take care of so many other children through our ministry. No matter what we've been through, we make an amazing team!

DEDICATION

You Raised Me—Dionisio Reyes Sr.

First of all, I dedicate this book to the first man that showed me the compassion to love someone that wasn't his own child, my dad—"Pop" Dionisio Reyes Sr. I grew up my whole life thinking that he was my biological father, only to find out in my forties, long after he had passed, that he was not. It was at that moment, when I was overwhelmed with emotion, that I came to the realization that this is where I got my heart to reach and love children that were not my own. I wished, at that moment, I could have given him the biggest hug and tell him, "Thank you!" Thank you, Pop!

You Helped Me—Chuck Jones

I dedicate this book to a man that took me in at a very difficult time in my life at sixteen years old. Chuck Jones told his wife Kim, "This is the Christian thing to do; we need to take in Louie." From that day forward, Chuck was such a spiritual influence and helped me finish high school. He was also the one that influenced me to join the United States Army. He said they would take care of me. The army did, and I learned so much how to be a man and a leader. Thank you, Chuck!

You Believed In Me—Dr. Mark Cowart

I dedicate this book to a man that believed in me at a pivotal time in my life as I began to really serve God as a young man. Pastor Mark Cowart became my pastor when I was twenty years old, and he took an interest in my life. He became my spiritual father and gave me a strong, spiritual foundation in my walk with the Lord. I am grateful that he gave me the opportunity to be in full-time ministry at a young age. Pastor Mark taught me so much about ministry while I was at his church, and today,

over twenty years later, he is still my pastor. Thank you,
Pastor Mark!

You Mentored Me—Pastor Bill Wilson

I dedicate this book to a man that helped me to see
that God can use anyone to do a great work for Him.
Pastor Bill Wilson helped me turn a vision God gave
me into a reality when I saw Pastor Bill's ministry and
saw that it could be done. Pastor Bill was doing what I
felt God called me to do but on a larger scale. The first
time I met him, he saw something in me, and years later,
he allowed me to travel with him to learn how to raise
support for the children; he mentored me on having
a ministry for at-risk children. I found out years later
that Pastor Bill doesn't just let anyone travel with him. I
am truly honored by this man and his heart to help me.
Thank you, Pastor Bill!

You Inspired Me—Pastor Willie George

I dedicate this book to a man that has inspired me
throughout my ministry career, Pastor Willie George.
Pastor Willie showed me how you can have an impactful
ministry for children and teenagers at a high level of
excellence. Pastor Willie was a man that turned the
body of Christ's heart to put a priority on the younger
generation. He inspired me not only to take our ministry
for the younger generation to another level but also to
write our own curriculum. Thank you, Pastor Willie!

ACKNOWLEDGMENTS

I WANT TO THANK the men and women of God that have gone before me that walked through the trenches and encouraged me to reach the next generation. These men and women of God have powerfully influenced my life and further shaped my heart for children and the young generation because their hearts were turned towards children.

- Pastor Mark Cowart
- Pastor Rod Parsley
- Pastor Willie George
- Pastor Bill Wilson
- Pastor Mike Bickle
- Mike Lassiter
- Norm Hewitt
- Jim Wideman
- Blaine Bartel
- Connie Schooler
- Lisa Dubois
- Holly Brower

I also dedicate this book to men all over the nation who are currently working with children; they are in the trenches everyday advocating for this young generation. I want to commend the men who are fathers that have not left their post and are still being a father to their children or a father to other children, for this is the spirit and the power of Elijah.

I want to thank all the children and teenagers of Sidewalk Sunday School/ Reach a Generation who allowed me to be a pastor and spiritual father to them. Because God wanted them reached, He equipped me to establish

Sidewalk Sunday School/Reach a Generation and advocate for children who were not mine, but who belong to the Lord.

I want to thank Shakrisha McClain and Travion Croft. The Lord gave me the opportunity to father you during a difficult time in your young lives, and you both taught me so much about fathering a fatherless generation. I am so glad that God used me during that challenging time in your lives to be a father to you. I will always love you and help you become all that God has called you to be.

I want to thank all of the teenagers who have given their time, energy, and talent as a part of our Teen Leadership Program. In the early years of our ministry, when there was no adult support, you were the backbone of our ministry, doing whatever it took to help me reach other children, as God sent me to travel around the nation raising support. You stayed back and helped run the ministry. Our ministry would not be established, successful, and filled with purpose today without the faithful and committed young people who helped run our sound system, cameras, lighting, and monitored buses and helped in classrooms! I'm so proud of you kids!

I want to thank my Bible college students for teaching me every day the responsibility I have as a spiritual father to help guide you, as young adults, into your destiny.

I know I could not be here today without our faithful and generous partners from across the nation. Thank you for believing in the vision God gave and standing with me all these years.

I am very grateful for the Church of Joy congregation. "In the power of all," you've sacrificed, served, and labored alongside of me, reaching this younger generation. Thank you for always funding the vision and making sure that a generation knows the Lord, and that children always have the opportunity to hear the gospel!

I am very grateful for my wonderful staff who has labored next to me through many challenging seasons and many wonderful seasons as well. You have worked so hard to help me reach this younger generation, whether is it through teaching, driving and fixing buses, leading worship, or just being an extension of me, reminding children that God has a plan for their lives. I know how you have sacrificed. Thank you for your faithfulness, loyalty, and commitment.

I would like to thank Dr. Ashley Harrell who helped contribute to this book and who has helped our ministry reach young people.

I would also like to thank Leilani Haywood for contributing to this book. She has really helped Reach A Generation with ongoing efforts.

I would like to thank Holly Brower, who was a missionary for Youth For Christ, sent to Waukegan, Illinois, to minister to us children. I am grateful she was courageous enough to go into an African American and Hispanic neighborhood, where I received Jesus Christ as my personal Lord and Savior when I was twelve years old.

I am truly grateful to Juanita Horton, who has labored with me from the very beginning. Juanita helped me do visitations with the children and shop at Sam's Club for the candy and snacks we gave every week. This woman did whatever it took to preach the gospel to the children in the early days before we ever had a staff. Thank you for standing with Tricia and me, believing in the vision, and never leaving when everyone else did. We are so glad you still serve with us and are a part of our lives.

I want to thank my friend, my associate pastor, and someone who is very dear to me, Jordan Jones. I've known you since you were a little child, as I was close to your family, and I am so proud of the man of God you've become. Thank you for all you do to ensure we have the best graphic design work and videos, and for standing with me in the spirit of Elijah, reaching this younger generation.

I truly appreciate Cheryl Williams who has stood with my wife and me from the beginning. Thank you for laboring with us in the early days; giving your counsel, prayer, and intercession; and supporting the mandate God has given me. You have been an amazing teacher of the Word and great facilitator of our Bible college. I know you have sacrificed with us all these years to be where we are today. We love and appreciate you, and we are glad that you too, never left, but stayed with us. Tricia and I are truly grateful for you.

CONTENTS

FOREWORD

I WILL NEVER FORGET the first time that I saw Louie Reyes in our church here in Colorado Springs in the fall of 1992. He was always well groomed, nicely dressed and had a seriousness about him that made him stand out in the crowd.

Over time I began to see the hand of God upon him in a very strong way as he began to volunteer in Children's Church and eventually come on full time staff as our Children's Church pastor. Then in 1997 we prayed over Pastor Louie and Tricia sending them out to pioneer and pastor a brand-new church and launch Sidewalk Sunday School in Waukegan, Illinois, where Pastor Louie grew up.

I cannot adequately express what a blessing it is to see the Lord's blessing that is upon their ministry. But that blessing did not come without a price. I had known of some of the pain of Pastor Louie's childhood, but as I read this book I learned of so much more that he had not shared with me.

It has been said that pain in our lives will either make us a monster or a minister. I am so thankful that Pastor Louie allowed the Lord to take his pain and turn his heart toward the children and make him into the minister that he has become today. Thousands of children have come to know and experience the love of God because of his obedience. I believe that a model has been and continues to be crafted by the Lord Himself that others will be able to draw from to reach children that are so dear to His heart. I encourage you to read with an open mind and allow the Lord to turn your heart to the children as well.

—Mark Cowart
Senior Pastor/Church For All Nations

Chapter 1

THE VISION

I envision this little boy standing on the corner. He's bare-chested with ripped up blue jeans. He's a black kid waiting to cross the street to the other side of the projects. He has a Chug-a Lug juice drink in his hand and a bag of chips. He's standing there, aimless and hopeless. Cars, church vans, buses, and luxury cars whiz by full of people who are dressed up, laughing, and smiling. The Lord speaks to me: "I want you to bring him to church."

I'M IN THIS trance-like vision in the projects on the south side of Waukegan. I'm walking down a narrow street in the projects having lived out that way. When you're out there alone, God talks to you. You have no one else to talk to, so God says, "Am I the only one who cares about these kids? There doesn't seem to be anyone else out here trying to reach all these children."

That little boy in the vision was a clear picture that no one was stopping to reach him. The people in this region were going to church and doing church, but missing that God wanted the younger generation reached. God was sending me back to the place I didn't want to go to reach kids like me. Here's how God called me and formed me to go back to the streets of Waukegan, Illinois, to build one of the largest children's ministries in the world from nothing.

THE BACK STORY

"Louie! Louie! Louie!" It seemed like my name was the only chorus in my mother's mouth that day as she came home from a hard day at the restaurant. Josephine, or Kitty as everyone called her, was only at the beginning of the constant song of my childhood, to run and do this or that at her beck and call because she worked too much and worked too hard, and I was just young enough to obey and old enough to do so quickly. "Louie, get in here and get this living room cleaned. And don't tell me that it ain't your stuff. All you kids need to help keep this place clean." Now in my heart I knew who "all you kids" meant, but I never saw that reality in who was there to help clean up or keep up or do what was necessary to make sure our big house on McAllister street stayed as nice as it was on the day we moved in. I was the one she called to start tasks and to keep things in order. My responsibility covered for the irresponsibility of or in the preoccupied busyness of others in my family, yet I was the youngest.

Our house was much larger than the family we were, just with Mom and Dad, my sister, Charmaine, and my brother, Denny. The two-story house in the middle of the south side of Waukegan was almost too perfect for us, with a basement to adventure in and a garage with a treasure trove of things to explore. There was something about that house, even in the midst of the daily yelling and screaming, that caused me to feel safe. Secure even. I felt safe and secure in the midst of chaos, and my youthful soul only knew to obey. I soon learned that my ability to do for others and not feel truly loved and affirmed allowed me to survive the torment of my life and my dysfunctional family in spite of my gnawing hunger for both.

I'm Louie, the youngest child of Dionisio and Josephine (Kitty) Reyes. Dionisio was a short Puerto Rican man with a slight frame, and my mom was a tall, stunning redhead who turned heads whenever she went outside, to my dad's consternation. They were complete opposites. Dad was calm, peaceful, and tranquil. Mom was a fiery, bold, outspoken, blunt woman. I was the last one to join the family after my older sister and my middle brother; my birth name is Luis, but Louie was a name that fit me.

As the youngest, there were so many things I had the unique vantage point of seeing. I was invisible as I watched cartoons on TV while the world of my family crashed around me. I was too young to understand at the time, but I'd eventually discover that family is not always like a "Leave it to Beaver" TV show and unlike the happy endings on Saturday morning cartoons. The hero doesn't always win, and there's not always a happily ever after.

In the midst of all that was happening around me, I had begun to feel the pain of poverty. My life was not what I was watching on TV. Instead of great family meals like on "The Brady Bunch," I spent many days hungry. My mom would tell us kids to go to our friend's house to eat because we didn't have any food. During the times when there was a box of cereal that lasted more than a week or so, I remember many times having to pick roaches out of my cereal and eating it with water. As a young child, that can make you pretty angry.

I was born in the summer of 1971, and my mom would tell me how, as a baby, I would not receive her nurture even when she attempted once to breastfeed me. I wonder if, as a baby, I sensed she really didn't want to nurture me. I can remember as far back as three and four years old yearning to lay on my mother, to receive her nurture. However, even then, she was very distant and cold. She wouldn't hold me the way a mother should for some reason. My longing for my mother's nurture negatively affected my view of women in a great way, and the blur of those early days comes into view when I discovered that the voice that soothed my fears belonged to my father, not my mother.

Dionisio Sr., or "Rey" as my mom called him, was a wonderful man. Somehow, I knew, from the core of who he was, he loved me. There was a depth in his eyes and a gentle smile that let me know that me just being me brought him joy. There is something about lighting up the eyes of a father. I have often wondered what he saw when he looked at me. Maybe I reminded him of his life long ago growing up on the island, during the mysterious unknown years long before he left Puerto Rico, joined the army, and married my mother. But it made me happy to see that little smile emerge on his warm, sand-colored face, a smile, just for me. "Louie," he would say, "everything will be fine. Everything will be OK." And for that moment, he was right.

Chapter 2

THE BATTLE BEGINS

Sometimes the most fearful things are the things we won't say, won't hear, and won't do. It's those things that rob us of our hope and our potential. Like a thief, fear draws a noose around reality and makes hope appear as a distant dream.

FOR SO MANY days, hope eluded me in the dark halls of my elementary school. Instead of being a place where I felt accepted and nurtured, the school was a battle zone where I often was the lone, resilient victor, left to resolve my anger and work through my pain. I remember it like it was yesterday, the feeling of Dad's chilly hand holding mine as we walked the long winding street down to my school. There was a crispness in the air, and I knew that no matter how hard I tried, something would happen that day that would make the anger rise—a look from a classmate, correction by the teacher, or a missed shot during a recess game—all were opportunities to unleash the anger that always seemed to simmer inside. But as I walked that morning, in silence with Dad, something in me hoped that today would be different.

I walked in the doors of Andrew Cooke School and saw the familiar faces, but something else was there too. Intimidation stood like a soldier in the corner waiting to take up its post in my heart. From the first moment of the daily lesson, intimidation blocked understanding, and fear caused unspoken questions to remain in my mouth unasked.

When the teacher asked who knew the answer, so often it wasn't me. Not because I was dumb, but because fear and intimidation had stolen my voice, and I soon learned that only anger could usurp them both. "Come on Louie, sit down. You need to behave....Turn around Louie, stop doing that....Ok, Louie, if you continue, I'm going to have to tell your dad...." The loosely veiled threats of my teacher did nothing to stem the impulsive battle I fought inside. I hated school. I hated that place that made me feel alone and unnerved, and if it took me being mean to others and being defiant to my teacher to get beyond the doors of the classroom, then I was willing.

On this particular day, Dad walked up the sidewalk to pick me up from kindergarten as he always did. Dad walked me to school in the morning on his way to work at Johns Manville's asbestos plant, and instead of eating, he'd use his lunch break to walk back to the school, pick me up, and take me home, only to repeat the trip before his meager lunch break expired. Then after work, he'd retrace his steps for the long walk home. But today, my teacher pulled my dad aside, shaking her head and showing him my papers, evidence of my defiance and unwillingness to follow her perfectly scripted classroom routine. Graciously, Dad nodded his head, looking toward me, and said, "I understand Louie; he'll be fine, but now we must go." We turned to leave, and the teacher stood speechless, not sure if her words had hit their target. "Wait, Mr. Reyes, there are things you must do...." But there was no waiting or returning. When we left the kindergarten classroom that afternoon, we walked out hand in hand, and never returned.

"For the rest of kindergarten, my education came from the teachers on the television screen in our family room."

From that day on, Dad woke me up in the morning as always and made sure I got at least a bowl of cereal before heading out the door to work at the John Manville plant. "Louie, don't open the door for anybody; I'll be back soon," he'd say through the door while locking it from the outside. And there I was, open to a new world of teachers on "Sesame Street," "The Electric Company," and cartoons. For the rest of kindergarten, my education came from the teachers on the television screen in our family room. The pressure was lifted, and I was relieved.

In those days, I found myself wondering and thinking about who I was and how I fit in my loud, often unstable family. Mom swept in like a rush of energy full of the days' trials with her apron pockets bulging from the tips she earned while working as a waitress during the day. I didn't know what it was then, but there was a restlessness about her where she was always looking for the next adventure. Beyond the perimeter of our front yard and the limitations of our south side neighborhood, there was something more exciting beckoning her. For Dad, there was a restfulness, a calm that was only interrupted when watching baseball on television or when something terrible happened in the news. Dad would rub my curly hair and then look off into the distance like he was dreaming of a future for me.

Mom left behind a few coins on the table for me and my brother to go to the corner store called People's Market. There was no end to the number of Now and Laters and Chico Sticks we'd love to buy, and we loved filling our cheeks with Mike & Ike's while running zig-zag through the alleys back to our house. There was something special about McAllister Street. For me it was the whole universe. Where else could you go and find the treasures that Denny and I discovered hidden behind dumpsters and tucked away in alleys? By the time the blistering days of July were in full force, we had an arsenal of junk that our neighborhood friends envied. Just when we though it couldn't get any better, Dad said, "We're moving!"

Moving for the Reyes family was a big deal. We weren't like the rich people on TV and we definitely didn't have fancy furniture or appliances from the department store, but we gathered what we had and moved from a rental on one side of the street to a home we owned on the other side of the street. Yes, that summer we moved from 831 McAllister to 832 McAllister, and I loved it! I think my brother and I had the most to gain out of the deal as we moved into a huge two-story home filled with the treasures of long gone owners who found their castoffs unworthy for their next journey. Not only would we find treasures inside, but my brother and I were speechless to discover the garage that had been left partially filled with tools and screws and anything a boy needed to get into just enough mischief to call it fun.

My brother and I shared a room together in the big house and my sister had her own room back by the kitchen. Mom and Dad had a room and there seemed to be room enough for us to welcome the entire neighborhood. As a matter of fact, we had an upstairs apartment that

Mom said would bring in extra cash for rainy days as soon as we found someone to rent the room.

I didn't know at the time how we got the house, but soon after moving in, Dad changed. He'd never return to work and the house became a foreboding sign of deteriorating security for us. I learned years later that we got the house that warm summer as a result of Dad's sickness. In his work at Johns Manville, he'd been exposed to asbestos and as a result his lungs and his life would never be the same. Unable to restore his ailing health, Johns Mansville offered a $20,000 settlement that was enough to secure a home for a family of five and offer an opportunity for a momentary leap into the life of abundance and stability. What I didn't know then was that new houses aren't necessarily home and stability is not something to take for granted.

Chapter 3

FROM COMPASSION TO ANGER

*The crackle of a belt stinging against skin scarred me
for life. Watching a defenseless young boy in the hands
of a mad man cast me into the role of a protector.*

THE BEST PART about moving and the summer before first grade was meeting Gerald. Gerald lived just behind our new house, across the alley in a falling-apart house. Gerald was different from anyone else I had ever known. He didn't know how to play baseball, and he didn't have any friends. He seemed scared and jittery all the time, and his big "owl-like eyes" filled with tears each time he got called into the house by a big man named John.

Gerald and I had adventures running through the neighborhood, me teaching him baseball and my favorite game, Strike Out, and him teaching me how to steal candy from the corner store. I discovered just how much candy I could stuff into one pocket if we stood in just the right position at the counter during the time it took for a family from the neighborhood to buy their evening groceries.

Gerald was short, with kinky black hair that was so different from mine. We must have looked strange hanging out together, but there was a deep bond that made our friendship stick from the start—Gerald knew I'd never hurt him.

I met Gerald when I was in the back of my new house throwing the ball in the air thinking of what it would be like to grow up and be a baseball player like Carlton Fisk. I noticed someone watching me through the chain link fence, and for a moment, I was startled. His piercing eyes never left the ball, as if he was mesmerized by it flying high in the afternoon sun. When I noticed him standing there, I forgot to catch and the ball rolled into a patch of deep grass.

Gerald responded instantly, running after the ball with ripped pants and tattered shoes. He reached for the ball and looked at me, waiting for permission to play. "Throw it!" I said, partially out of impatience and partially out of selfish fear. "Throw it to me!" Gerald paused for a minute and then threw the ball awkwardly as if he had never done so before.

I was shocked because he threw like a girl! But the embarrassed look on his face told me that it wasn't that he didn't want to throw it the right way, he didn't know how. So I grabbed the ball from the edge of the alley, and instead of continuing to play alone, I tossed it low and slow. Even though he missed it, he smiled and laughed. And for a while, we played like that, tossing, running, and learning in the alley until that perfect afternoon of new friendship was interrupted by a rage I'd never knew existed.

"Without a word, Big J cast Gerald and me into two roles
that I never resented, Gerald was my friend and Big J's
victim, and I was Gerald's friend and protector."

"Gerald, you little no good for nothing, where are you? I told you to stay in the house and now you're going to pay!" A huge man, I will call him Big J, the live-in boyfriend of Gerald's mom, stumbled out of the house cursing, red-eyed, and drunk. He roared with anger as he screamed Gerald's name repeatedly, spiked with profanity for everyone to hear.

Not knowing what to do, I ran to hide. Gerald wasn't so lucky. Stuck, motionless like a statue, Big J lunged over him with an endless brown belt and silver belt buckle that he lashed across Gerald's back and head for more times than I care to count. I flinched with every crackle of the belt that snapped against his bare flesh. Gerald sobbed and whimpered as he crumbled to the ground under Big J's lashes.

Without a word, Big J cast Gerald and me into two roles that I never resented, Gerald was my friend and Big J's victim, and I was Gerald's friend and protector. We never talked much about the beatings Gerald took from Big J. When Gerald winced in pain as he threw the ball, or on days when he wanted to just sit in the shade instead of running through the maze of our neighborhood, I knew he had been beaten.

Gerald and I ran the streets and alleys and rummaged in my garage a lot during that first summer. There was always an adventure and baseball and just enough bottles to cash in to get something sweet from the neighborhood grocery store, MB Foods. When Gerald's family struggled because their electricity or water was shut off, and they had no food for weeks, our adventures of stealing food and candy softened the bleak reality of the constant hunger and neglect. I had a lot of compassion for Gerald; I knew he was poor like me, but I began to realize he was a lot poorer than I was. So, in the winter I would rummage through the lost and found at school and find Gerald gloves, hats, and coats so he had something to keep him warm.

Though my friendship with Gerald was special, the first kid I met on the south side of Waukegan was a boy named Rodney and his older brother Leroy. Rodney and Leroy filled in the spaces that my brother left open, and it was the two of them that taught me how to play baseball. We had so many fun sunny days, lost in our own world, playing Strike Out in the alleys and our own version of major league ball at King Park.

Rodney and Leroy's house was different from mine. Their mom and dad had well-paying jobs, and even though they weren't flashy enough to make me feel bad, I knew that they had more than me. Whenever a new toy or a new style came out, Leroy and Rodney always had it first. I can remember the wonder of watching movies on their VCR and playing video games on their Atari Game system. For a kid like me, going to their house was like going to another planet, a world where money was something adults worried about, and a kid could just focus on being a kid.

The soft breeze of August days came, and with it, an expectation that I'd start school again. Big school, this time, as Mom called it. "No more school with the TV, Louie; you're going to go out there and really learn something." Although I'd never admit it, I was scared. I didn't want to go back to that place, so far from the comfort of my home and so filled with rules of do's and don'ts, can'ts and won'ts. I was used to the rhythm of my house with Dad's early mornings, Mom's late nights, and my brother and sister's arguing. Nevertheless, the end of summer eventually arrived and excitement filled the neighborhood like thunderclouds before a storm. Everyone was preparing for the new school year, and I knew that I'd have to try again.

First grade started well with new faces, new teachers, new games, and new play places, but eventually the newness faded and the reality of school life began to settle in. There were moments I loved, like hearing an afternoon story read from the big book and getting lost in the details of storybook adventures, but then there were moments I dreaded. I never liked sitting at my desk, chained to worksheets and questions that seemed to appear without end. I got tired of sitting there trying to care about vowels and consonants, counting coins, and tracing patterns; instead, in frustrated silence, I was angry.

Sometimes I'd just stare ahead, refusing to do anything, hoping that the endless string of math problems would fade away. At other times, I'd tear the papers to shreds, making it impossible to complete the jumbled mess. Still at other times, the worst times, I'd make sure to let my teacher know that no one, and I mean no one, could make me do anything I didn't want to do.

11

It was a gloomy winter afternoon and my teacher offered a trade as she had so many times before. "Louie, if you don't do your work, there will be no recess for you. You won't leave that chair until every blank is filled!" Her ultimatum seemed to satisfy her, but for me it was like lighting a powder keg. Something shot through me like a lightning rod and before I knew what happened, the desk was flipped over, and I was punching, kicking, fighting, and biting my teacher. Never mind that she was bigger than me. Never mind that I might get in trouble. Never mind that the other kids in the room had become paralyzed in fear. I was overcome by a rage that I couldn't control, but I remember desperately wishing someone could help me.

Chapter 4

RAGE LIKE A VOLCANO BEGINS TO ERUPT

Labels can either limit you or push you to freedom.
Being called the bad kid, when I wanted to be good,
created resentment that fueled uncontrollable anger. I
had to learn, somehow, to control my anger.

THE SCHOOL DISTRICT sent a man I called Mr. K to see me once a week. I actually liked him. We went to his classroom and talked about baseball and school. We played games, and he asked me about what made me happy and sad, excited or mad. I didn't really like the time that he made me look at the cards full of blurry ink and his endless way of asking me what I saw. That was the only day I got mad at Mr. K, and he never made me do that again.

School was a daily trial for the teachers and me, to see who would win first in our battle of wills and in the rage of my anger. None of us ever knew what set me off, but there was a split second before I lost control. The adrenaline that pumped through my veins overshadowed any logic, and the only language I spoke was translated into throwing chairs, flipping desks, and striking out at whoever got too close. Before long, I had a reputation for being a bad kid. Dumb. Out of control. Hopeless. Lost. And in those days, for kids like me, there was special education.

In special education, I lost my name, and I became a label: hyper, unmanageable, unteachable, and impossible.

The strange thing about special education was that there was nothing special about it. I soon discovered that my anger gave me access into a world that was more concerned with what I had done to others instead of being concerned about how to help me. In special education, I lost my name, and I became a label: hyper, unmanageable, unteachable, and impossible. I regularly ignored a teacher's command in an outburst of uncontrollable anger that followed the scripts of these labels. I decided that school wasn't the place for me and while I had to be there, the only thing that brightened my day was the time I spent with my friend Gerald, who liked me just the way I was and who never tried the complicated task of teaching me anything.

On bad days, the principal called my mom to the school, and she'd give me a look that said, in some way, that she understood how I was feeling. Though she never told me that my outbursts were acceptable, Mom didn't punish me after days that I struggled to settle down and learn. Years later, I realized that my Mom had her own outbursts of anger and consoling me in my own anger was her way of saying, "I know what you're going through."

When we got home, she let me have dinner early. Sometimes I'd get to eat my favorite breakfast cereal for dinner, as if she somehow tried to add some sweetness to the rottenness of the day. Eventually, the school decided that there was something really wrong with me. Even though I tried, I never figured out how to get the teachers to leave me alone.

There was always a pressure to be different from who I was. There was always a ribbon or a gold star for the kid who had all the answers right, or the one who knew all the spelling words, or even worse, for the one who knew just how to say their math facts in front of everyone out loud. I wasn't that kid. I was a kid who loved Franken Berry and Boo Berry cereal every morning and who could live to watch Carlton Fisk play for the White Sox. I was pretty simple—cereal and baseball.

The volume was turned up too high on every conversation in our house that ended with slamming doors and unsettling nights.

School didn't allow my life to stay simple. Things got more and more complicated for me every year. By second grade, teachers knew to watch out for me, and my temper, and as school got more difficult, I had more reasons to be angry. I hated how I felt, and I didn't know how to control my emotions. My teachers had become my victims of biting, hitting, and angry outbursts. They didn't know how my life had changed. Now that Dad wasn't working, the life that used to be in his eyes only flickered out into mundane days of waiting to see how many tips my mom brought home. Mom, now the sole breadwinner, hated her new role; she constantly screamed at my dad about how much the kids cost—to feed, clothe, and keep a roof over their heads. The volume was turned up too high on every conversation in our house that ended with slamming doors and unsettling nights.

As my brother and sister got older, they came home less and less, and no one seemed to mind. "One less mouth to feed and one less kid to hear," Mom said, as she put her exhausted feet up on the coffee table in the darkened living room.

Days and nights like these taught me that I could never talk about money.

I realized that everything in our home was based on how much money we had, or didn't have. Whenever my brother and sister asked for money, the air got tight, and it seemed like I couldn't breathe. There was never enough, and it didn't seem that Mom could work enough hours to pay the pile of bills and buy groceries, clothes, and supplies that we needed.

So, when I returned to school each year, there were no new school supplies, lunchboxes, backpacks, pencils, or folders. There was no money. I couldn't ask. Fighting back embarrassment and shame, I'd return to school with last year's supplies and those Gerald and I had stolen from other kids' abandoned lockers and desks the year before, crumpled and used in a grocery store bag.

At first with Gerald, it didn't seem so bad. We shared what we had together. Then there were the stares and snickers of my classmates with their shiny lunchboxes and fancy new folders with cartoon characters and superheroes on front. They didn't know what we felt. They didn't care that my crayons worked just as well as theirs even though the packages were ripped and the tips worn down after a prior year's use.

Even my friend Rodney didn't understand. Though he never made me feel bad, it was hard not to compare my worn out clothes and school supplies to the stylish clothes he wore to start a new school year. Part of me wished we were more than friends. An aching wonder began in my soul. What did it feel like to be cared for completely? What does it feel like to have what you need, even without stealing it? For me, poverty began to follow me to school and gave me even more of a reason to feel alone and out of place.

FIRST ENCOUNTER

Kids weren't the only ones who let me know I didn't fit. With my light skin, and curly kinky hair, the Black kids reminded me that I was different and the White kids let our obvious differences speak for themselves. Here I was the son of a White woman and a Puerto Rican man in a predominately Black neighborhood, and in the 1980s, there weren't many kids who looked like me. I had to learn quickly how to defend myself, and after a few fights I realized my mixed ethnicity would always have to be defended. Strangely enough, the isolation of who I was never really got to me. I learned quickly that I could have friends, but I had better not really rely on anyone other than myself. I learned not to care much what others thought, and I was comfortable that way. I liked being in control, especially in school, when everything seemed so rigid and routine.

On some days, I had quiet moments alone at my home. My imagination was free as I tinkered on my bike in the garage or threw my baseball as hard as I could against the garage door. On those days, I was thinking and dreaming about what the future might hold for a kid like me. On a sunny but not too hot day, as I perched on a crate in the garage to fix a flat tire on my bike, time stood still as the light shone in from the small window on the other side of the garage. Although I wasn't afraid, I knew I wasn't alone, and I saw a glowing book appear in the window, open, and then disappear almost as quickly as it had appeared.

I didn't know it then, but at eight years old, it was the first of many times that the Lord would make His presence known to me. I felt like an invisible person was standing behind me. This presence gave me goose bumps, and chills ran up and down my arm. I felt vulnerable, and emotions that I didn't know were there stirred deep within. All I knew then was that I didn't have to fear how I felt that day, and for some reason my life wouldn't be the same.

Summer days became a blur of baseball, South Side adventures, and stolen sweets from the People's Market on Lincoln and 8th Street by the time I realized it was time to return to school. By the first week of the fourth grade, I was sitting in the class of a teacher who I'm sure hated me. She's probably heard for years how I had caused problems in other classes and maybe she decided she'd be the one to lay down the law.

Her steely stare bore into me on the first day of class as she went over rules such as like staying in our chairs and using supplies in our classroom. With every remark, her eyes focused on me as if I needed extra emphasis to be sure I got the point. I knew instantly that I was in for a long year. Mr. K. wasn't around anymore to talk things out, and I knew the principal would never take my side on things. I knew that if I ever really lost my temper, things would go from bad to worse pretty fast.

A rage that had been building up inside
me started to erupt like volcano.

Fourth grade started fine as we learned multiplication facts and making fractions, and I secretly enjoyed figuring out the answers to the math flashcards during drills with a partner. I felt good about myself; even though math was hard, I started understanding it. One cool afternoon in early November, however, those same math problems became the beginning of everything falling apart.

This time, we weren't working with partners; we were working alone on a difficult set of worksheets that I didn't understand. I leaned over to ask my friend for help, but almost in an instant, my teacher stuck her finger in my face and her voice got louder as she accused me of cheating. She didn't listen to me explain as she went on and on about how much trouble I was in and what a bad influence I was.

I tried to stay quiet for as long as I could, but I knew that I had to do something to make her stop. Before I realized it, I stood up and threw my desk across the room. I lunged at my teacher to stop her from saying such terrible things about me. A rage that had been building up inside me started to erupt like volcano. For the first time, I gave up hope of ever having control of it.

Chapter 5

A NINE YEAR OLD IN HANDCUFFS?

Steel handcuffs cutting into my arms at nine-years-old taught me that I never wanted to be handcuffed again. The storm inside that spilled out to the class needed to be contained. I wanted so badly for someone to get me under control!

I COULD HEAR MYSELF screaming at her, but inside, the loudest voice was the one telling me how much I wished this was over. By the time the principal came to rescue my teacher, everything became a blur as I swung toward her again and again, fighting now for survival. The principal managed to get me out of the classroom and we struggled down the hall, me yelling and the principal muttering obscenities through clenched teeth.

In his hurry to be rid of me, he pushed me into his office, closed the door and locked it from the outside. There we were, me on one side of the door and he on the other. The loud click of the lock made me feel like a caged animal. I had to get out of there and I didn't care about consequences. Like a mighty tornado, I kicked the chairs across the room and flipped the principal's paper-covered desk over with a strength that I didn't know I possessed.

I couldn't stop, I wanted the principal and everyone else to feel the pain that I felt at having to be scolded again and again, mocked and rejected, alone and ashamed. And like something out of a movie, the police were there suddenly—holding me, restraining me, grabbing me with their calloused hands and rough voices. Soon enough my face was planted in the corner of the principal's office as I was handcuffed behind my back. I was nine years old, and I wanted so badly for someone to get me under control.

My anger took me on a journey that I didn't want to go on, and the cold, tight steel handcuffs from that officer's waist got me back on track.

"It wasn't my fault," I wailed. But everyone was done listening to my excuses, and no one was ready to hear the truth from me. I fought to catch my breath as they left me standing there. By the time my jagged breaths subsided, I thought about the only person who loved me enough and who listened long enough to hear my side of the story. I thought of my dad. I thought of good memories and times we had together. I thought of that day about a year and a half before when my dad woke me up early one Saturday morning to go fishing at the lake in McHenry County.

At 5:00 a.m., he nudged me awake. Even though I was half-asleep, I didn't want to miss out on a fun day of fishing. My brother didn't wake up, and I was thankful that I had Dad all to myself. I fell asleep in the back seat of the car during the hour-long ride to the lake. The sun peeked over the trees surrounding the lake, and I began to get more and more excited as I helped Dad take the supplies out of the car. The fishing was slow, but I had a great day with Dad, listening to stories of his childhood in Puerto Rico and hearing what it was like for him as a soldier in the US Army. After a few hours, I got hungry, and I begged Dad to buy a pizza from the Snack Shack at the top of the hill instead of eating the sandwiches we brought from home. He smiled gently and counted out the money for me to buy a pizza. I was so excited. I ran up the hill and ordered a pepperoni pizza for Dad and me. The pizza felt warm through the open box as the cashier handed it to me through the window.

I was so excited as I began carrying it down the slope to where Dad stood fishing, but the bottom of the box began to get hotter and hotter, and my feet couldn't move fast enough. Suddenly, I tripped and fell, landing on top of the steaming pizza. I stood up crying with red splotches across my shirt, more upset by the spoiled pizza than by the pain of the hot cheese where it had burned my chest.

Dad walked up the rest of the hill and quickly wiped the remaining sauce from my hands and face. I was defeated and embarrassed because I knew that Dad really didn't have enough money to buy the first pizza, and I was still really hungry. Dad reached for my hand and we walked back up the hill together, and I stood in awe as he paid for a second pepperoni pizza.

This time, his strong hands held the pizza as we walked over to the picnic tables and sat down together, enjoying the pizza in silence. On that day, like no other, I knew how much he really loved me. It was that feeling that I reached for now, after three hours of standing in that corner, hands cuffed behind my back, hearing them decide whether to kick me out of school.

I began to daydream again and wished Dad was there. Somehow, no matter how bad things got, Dad always made sure I was all right.

Chapter 6

CONFINED TO A CUBE

*Everyone has something special that separates him
from others. For me, it is my ability to learn cruel
lessons at the hands of unfortunate circumstances. At
a very young age, I learned to be a man.*

AFTER THE POLICE encounter and incident in my classroom, I never went back. I returned to school, but I never went back to that class. Actually, they came up with a punishment that would make regular suspension look like a field trip. After spending a week at home, I went back to school and the janitor met me at the front door. I had never talked to him before, but with a wave of his hand he said, "Follow me."

I followed him down the winding hall back to a hidden door that I had never seen before. He swung the door open wide to reveal a wood shop with planks of wood leaning against the wall. As I hesitated at the door, he said, "It's for you; come help me." So for the next three days, I'd go to the wood shop with the janitor to build a place for me. At first, I didn't know what it was, but eventually I discovered that I wasn't welcome in any classroom.

The school janitor and I built a cubical desk that sat outside of the principal's office for me, every day from that day forward. By the end of the week, the cubical was in place and a mound of worksheets and books lay waiting for me. The cube became my classroom for the next year.

Cube Confinement

I sat at that cube every day, from 7:45 in the morning until 3:00 in the afternoon, day in and day out. While students were receiving instruction from their teachers, I was left to myself to work through a pile of meaningless worksheets and books. I was glad to be away from my scowling teacher that called me a bad kid. The worst part, however, was watching the other kids walk by on their way to gym and music, recess and lunch, pointing and laughing. No one cared.

There was no one to answer my questions if I got stuck on a problem on my worksheet. There was no one to guide me or instruct me. The newly learned math skills I started to learn in fourth grade became a vague memory and to this day, I've never learned how to properly multiply or understand fractions. I was a nuisance and a necessary burden to the school. I was the bad kid.

During those days, I lived for weekend baseball games in the Bronco Baseball League, hanging out with Gerald, and finding enough bottles to return to the corner store to buy rubber baseballs from the 7-Eleven. I fell into a routine of doing my schoolwork in my cube all day, and then eating whatever Dad decided to cook for dinner.

Near the end of fourth grade, I noticed that Mom wasn't home as much. She'd come in after working as a waitress, shake a few coins out of her apron and grab a new dress from the closet for work the next day. I didn't understand what was going on between her and my dad. They were becoming invisible to one another, not speaking, not listening, and not living. Then, for about two weeks, she was gone.

When Mom left the first time, I missed her. There was something about the way her broad shoulders shook when she laughed, or the way she tilted her head back on the couch after a long day of waiting tables. I missed the way her voice seemed to fill up a room even when she wasn't really talking about anything important. I missed my mom. In the two weeks that she was gone, I missed her cooking the most.

Dad's constant menu of spaghetti, rice, and beans made me long for the spicy dishes that Mom prepared. Though I tried to be grateful, her absence made me long for her dishes even more. When I finally asked my dad where she was, he replied, "She's gone to play Bingo." I didn't know what that meant really, but I nodded as if I understood and continued eating the meager evening meal in silence.

> Looking back now, I wonder if Mom made the meal
> to make us happy, to somehow make up for the time
> she spent away—living another life without us.

At the end of the second week, I was surprised to see her walk through the front door flushed and anxious, as if she was returning from some great adventure. "Hey, Louie, don't just stand there. Help me with these bags!" Too excited to ask where she'd been, I grabbed the bags and smiled with delight at the fixings for my favorite meal of bacalao and cabbage. Bacalao is a Puerto Rican meal of salted codfish that makes your mouth water even with the thought of it.

Looking back now, I wonder if Mom made the meal to make us happy, to somehow make up for the time she spent away—living another life without us. Regardless of the intent, it was a special day: Mom was back, she made a special meal, and things were back to "normal," at least for the time being.

I don't know if my sister and brother missed her as much as I did. As a teenager, my sister was more interested in what was going on with her friends and boyfriends than anything in our house. Maybe Mom's absence gave her a reason to isolate herself; she never talked to me.

We didn't get along and our relationship was reduced to awkward occasional meals at dinner and me pretending not to notice how often she slipped in late through the back door of the house on her way to her bedroom. By this time, my relationship with my brother wasn't much different. We weren't the same partners in adventure that we had been only a few years before when we first moved into our new home on McAllister Street.

My brother and I used to play baseball and go fruit hunting. Our neighborhood was full of pear, apple, and cherry trees. We had cut down a neighborhood apple tree together. As that tree fell down at our feet, I remember the peaceful moment of achieving something together, with my big brother.

Once when we were spear fishing on Lake Michigan, we saw a giant school of fish. We both threw our spears at the biggest fish and hit it in the head. The fish was three and a half pounds, and we couldn't haul it home on our bikes. We hid the fish under the dock and rode our bikes home to get Dad. Dad drove us back, and the fish was still there underneath the dock. We brought the fish home.

I missed raiding neighbor's gardens with him and stealing rhubarbs. The long nights of playing baseball in the alleys or football in the streets with our friends began to fade away. The more we fought, those hot summer days of catching the bus to Belvidere Mall to play video games had ended.

Now we had become contentious, the lines drawn between what was his and what was mine. Since he was a couple of years older, my brother's friends wanted nothing to do with me and to be honest, I didn't mind. My brother was different from me—more concerned about nice clothes and shoes and impressing the girls. He worked a lot on cars. I didn't care about those things. As long as I had baseball, everything was fine.

My brother and sister weren't there when Mom first came home, and I was thankful for time alone with her. As she stood at the sink rinsing the cabbage, emotion welled up in me as I sat on the chair facing the stove. "Mom, I really missed you," I said. "Things are different when you're not here. I'm so glad you're back." Mom turned and looked at me with a strange look in her eyes. "Louie, I'm surprised to hear you say that," she said. "You don't need anybody. You've never needed me." Instantly a wall was raised between us—a wall that separated me from being vulnerable to her, or anyone—a wall that pushed me into the pain of becoming a man too soon, feeling somehow orphaned in spite of my mother's presence in the room. Before the tears fell that welled in my eyes, I found my way to my room, to push down the feelings of shame and embarrassment that threatened to choke me.

I lay across my bed trying to understand the invisible scar that etched into my heart and fell asleep before discovering a salve to cover the wound. For a few days after that, I was quiet. No baseball. No bike rides through the neighborhood. No adventures with Gerald. Something in me had been broken, and I didn't know how to heal. Looking back now, I know that my mom was trying, in her own way, to make me strong and to prepare me for the days ahead. More important than what she said is the lesson I learned about the power of words and how one word can change everything.

In the weeks after Mom's return, the muggy nights of summer covered the South Side like a blanket. Without air conditioning, the best way to cool off was just to relax across my bed, trying to be as still as possible until the whirring fan pushed out the oppressive heat. There was a lot of commotion among the neighbors because of the influx of new residents. The neighborhood had changed for the worse, from a lower-middle class area to simply a low class area with the new residents that brought their poverty, despair, and desperation with them.

After a while, we knew that we couldn't go to McAllister Grocery Store after dark because of the dangerous gang activity. By nightfall, the streets of the South Side were transformed into a war zone and being in the wrong place at the wrong time meant the difference between life and death.

In 1980, my life was dominated by baseball during the day and avoiding getting into a fight or running into a shootout with the violence that ruled the streets at night.

Chapter 7

SKEEZIE'S BEEN SHOT

Seeing a teen boy, someone I knew, take his last breath would change my life forever. The reality of where I lived, the gang violence, I was one choice away from that destructive life.

I WAS IN BED, falling asleep to the sound of the oscillating fan and Dad listening to the evening news when my sister burst in the front door screaming, "Skeezie's been shot! Skeezie's been shot!" I bolted out of bed and followed my brother out the front door to see Skeezie laying down in a pool of blood just a few feet from our house. Skeezie was a sixteen-year-old boy that everyone knew in the neighborhood. He was likeable and funny, and strangely enough, not in a gang. It was horrible.

Someone had turned him over on his back, and he looked up at the sky with fear in his eyes. He began to mumble, something that I couldn't hear or understand at first. Then, before he closed his eyes, the last words I heard him say were, "Go get my mama." Suddenly, the entire neighborhood was outside. Someone ran toward Skeezie's house, which was only two blocks away. I stood there still, terrified, and afraid. I'd heard gunshots before, I'd seen bullets before, but I would never forget the night that I watched Skeezie take his last breath and die. The anguished expression on his face and cry for his mom was worse than any horror movie I'd ever seen.

That night, Skeezie wasn't the only one who didn't make it home. His classmate lay dying further down the street, saying her own goodbyes after being shot by the same angry hand that took Skeezie's life. This teenage girl was my sister's best friend, and her death hit my sister hard. She and Skeezie were both shot by this teenage boy because of drama between them. The senseless killings and the influx of violence in my neighborhood confirmed that the familiar streets of the South Side would never be the same for me.

I went to bed that night, thinking about how in his last moments, Skeezie called for his mom. Then I thought about my own family: Dad—quietly struggling to breathe, passing the days with medications and television; Mom—strong and beautiful, yet untouchable and unstable; my sister—resilient, rebellious, and removed. If I called for her, would she come? My brother—different and distant; not the friends in adventure we once were. Who would I call? Who would come for me? I fell asleep still wondering, *whom could I call? Who really cared for me?*

The summer eventually faded into fall and it was time to enter school again. I dreaded it more than ever, and I made up my mind that I wouldn't lose control this year. I could survive the eight hours I spent there each day. On the first day of classes, the principal met me at the front door with a smile and said, "Come on, Louie."

As I followed him down the hall, there it was, as terrible as the year before. The cube sat in front of the principal's office, solemnly, as if it knew that I would return to its solitude and its shame. I fought back tears as I quietly took my seat. I put my head down as I prepared myself for the taunts of my classmates and the jeers of my baseball teammates as they went through the halls on their way to gym, recess, music, and the library.

Fifth grade was a sequel to the nightmare of fourth grade. I knew that this wasn't the time to get angry; something had to change. My anger built the cube, and I needed to find a way out of the cube and back into the classroom with my friends. Over the course of the first few months of fifth grade, I sat in that cube every day, struggling through my work, but spending a lot of time sorting things out in my head—thinking about Mom and Dad, my sister and my brother, old friends like Gerald and new friends I'd made, like Dax.

During fifth grade, I got a job delivering newspapers to pay for food and clothes that my family couldn't afford to buy. I woke up at 5:00 a.m. every day and while my classmates were sleeping, I rode my bike from house to house delivering newspapers in the frigid cold during the winter. When I rode my bike down dark streets under dim street lamps, I wondered how it felt to be able to sleep in a warm bed and not have to worry about what you're going to eat that day or if you had clean clothes to wear to school.

I knew that there was something very different about me—I couldn't put my finger on it, but I felt it. Even though I liked having others around, I couldn't let myself need them or depend on them anymore. I didn't know if this was what being a man felt like, but somehow the awestruck wonder of being a kid watching cartoons had finally worn off, and I couldn't ignore the grim reality of how poverty and neglect defined my life, my family, and even school.

Chapter 8

KITTY AND BASEBALL!

For some reason, my mom came back during that season we needed a baseball coach. Maybe God knew I needed that, to see she cared or maybe to keep baseball in my life. I was good at baseball, and it became my lifeline to staying off the streets and out of trouble.

AFTER THE FIRST time that Mom went away and came back, our family fell apart on the inside, and the house showed signs of neglect too. The screen in our door was torn, the lights flickered occasionally, and water leaked from the sink. The hardwood floors creaked as you walked from one side to the other. The leak under the sink got worse because Dad was physically unable to repair the pipe, and we didn't have the money to pay a plumber. We did what other families in our neighborhood did and put a bowl underneath the leaky sink. We ignored the obvious signs of gray-green patches of mold in the basement, a broken window, and weeds overtaking our yard. The new house we bought that was supposed to change everything began to look like the neighborhood we lived in. It was falling apart. Poverty took over; life was getting worse, not better.

I gathered milk crates from the grocery store dumpster, two at a time, to create a dresser to hold my clothes in the room my brother and I shared. In colors like red and orange, I stacked the crates on top of one another with their open sides facing out, to transform them into a place for my clothes, socks, and personal items. I was thankful to have a bed. I was thankful to have clothes for the crates. I was thankful to have so much more than my friend Gerald, even if it didn't amount to much. One of the best things about survival is that it breeds creativity, perseverance, and gratitude, which pops up at unexpected times.

As baseball season in the Bronco League got started that year, I was so excited. Mom had followed me down to the ball field to fill out the papers that parents had to sign, and she lingered by the bleachers, talking to some of the other mothers and fathers. After a few moments, the league director gathered everyone and thanked us for coming. He talked about all the practices and the Saturday morning games, when he stopped abruptly and said, "Uh, but we do have a problem that I'm hoping one of you parents can help us with. We have a coach for everyone else, but we need a coach for the Mustangs."

There was silence. "Oh, no," I thought, "that's my team. If we don't have a coach, we can't play. What will we do?" And before I could worry any further, a familiar voice from behind me piped up, "I'll do it. It can't be that hard…"

It was my mother, yes! Josephine "Kitty" Reyes was the new coach of my baseball team! My White, redheaded mom would coach a bunch of Black kids and me in Little League Baseball! I don't know what she was thinking, but I was thankful for her that day. Provision can come from some pretty surprising places, and for me and for baseball, I didn't care who coached as long as I could play short-stop.

For some reason, my mom didn't run off during that season we needed a coach. Maybe God knew I needed that, to see she cared or maybe to keep baseball in my life. I found out that I was good at baseball, and it became my lifeline to staying off the streets and out of trouble.

Mom and Dad were at every baseball game. During one game, Mom cussed out the referee so bad that everyone listening was glad he or she wasn't him. Her creative use of profanity made the man cringe before her. She could coax a hit out of a mediocre player with her unforgettable encouragement. After the games, Mom and Dad hosted after parties that didn't show our lack as they served hamburgers, candy, and soft drinks. They pulled together the team, and we had a good time, even if we lost the game. Mom and Dad also met my new friend, Dax's, parents, Chuck and Kim.

Because of baseball, I spent a lot more time with my friend Dax than I did with Gerald. Dax was a baseball player that anyone would love to have on his team. Even as a kid, Dax was stronger, faster, and more talented than the rest of us. He never made us feel bad about it, but we were proud that he was on our team, especially when he whacked the ball high over the fence for a home run. Dax was also a great friend.

My relationship with him was different from my relationship with Gerald. With Gerald, we found ourselves locked into our own world of running through the alleys and finding things to do in the neighborhood.

Gerald didn't fit in with kids like Dax, and though he was never mistreated, he was never accepted. Dax and I had a lot in common. Even though he was older than I was by a year or so, he was the only person I knew that loved baseball more than I did. He could tell you stats and stories about all of the baseball greats, and he'd set up a play in the middle of a Strike Out game that made you feel like you were in the big leagues. I can remember fun times that I had at Dax's house. Like me, he lived in Waukegan, but he wasn't the youngest. He was actually the oldest with a little sister named Bethany. Their home was nicer than ours, and the atmosphere was peaceful and orderly.

One night after a baseball game, I went to Dax's house and his mom, Kim, was making dinner in the kitchen. She seemed happy, smiling even as she put together the meal for the family. Dax said that his mom was having two more babies soon, since they had just found out she was pregnant with twins. Dax's dad, Chuck, worked a lot, but he always made time to throw the ball around with us in the back yard whenever I came over to visit.

Dax's family was different from mine, and there was something about their difference that I missed at home with my own family. One night after baseball practice, he said he didn't want to go home because it was Family Night. "What's that?" I asked. He sighed, threw the ball up in the air, and said, "Oh it's when we play games and talk about the Bible." Families playing games together? This was such a foreign concept that I had to see this for myself. My concept of family was everyone who did their own thing. When they were in the same house, they were screaming at each other. "Can I go?" I asked.

He looked at me closely, like I was an alien. "Seriously? You want to go Family Night?"

"Yeah!" I said.

"Well, I'll go if you go," he said. When I walked in the door, Kim was surprised to see me. Chuck beckoned me to the table. Dinner was ready, and they set down another plate.

After dinner, Kim cleared the table, and Chuck pulled out the Bible. He talked about knowing God, how we can know Him and follow Him. I had never heard God talked about in a family setting unless His name was used in a curse word. Dax looked bored and watched my reaction. He expected me to snicker and tell his dad, "Thank you, but can we do something that is really fun?"

Instead, to Dax's surprise, I asked Chuck how he knew that heaven was real. Chuck was shocked, and he smiled as he shared some of the scriptures about heaven in the Bible. I wasn't satisfied that he knew the scriptures. I wanted to know if Chuck thought heaven was real. Chuck then said, as I was sitting in front of him, that heaven was real to him. I never forgot that for the rest of my life.

I asked more questions while Dax wandered away and turned on the TV. I forgot the time as Chuck and Kim answered my questions. Then Kim looked at the clock and thought it was too late for me to ride my bike back to my house. "Chuck, you need to drop him off," she said. When Chuck drove me home, we parked outside in front of the house. I didn't want to get out of his car because I felt safer in his car than in my home. You didn't know what was going to happen when you walked through the doors of my house, who was going to be fighting.

After answering more of my questions about God, Chuck said he thought it was getting late and that my mom and dad must be worried about me. "I need to go, Louie," he said. "I have to get up early for work tomorrow."

"OK, Mr. Jones! Can I come back over again for family night?" I asked.

"Of course you can come," he said.

By mid-year, others must have noticed the change in me. After Christmas break, I came back to school and the cube was gone.

Chapter 9

UNEXPECTED GIFTS

A mistake or surprise can bring the most unexpected gift. You can find something positive in any situation, even if it starts out as a mistake.

THE CUBE WAS no longer parked in front of the principal's office like an unavoidable eyesore for everyone to see. I was confused at first, but then the principal's secretary quietly walked me down the hall where the fifth graders were already in class. "Good luck Louie; be good," she said as she gently knocked on the door, and the fifth grade teacher answered. I went in, wondering if this was a joke. But no, after over a year, I was back with my classmates—no longer ridiculed, no longer rejected. I had another chance, and I wasn't going to take it lightly.

Looking back now, I realize that it's not the big decisions that make the greatest differences in our lives. The small choices that we make open doors of opportunity, re-establish trust, and restore hope. I learned to choose to do my work quietly or to not be angry. I could choose to cooperate with teachers that labeled me as the hyper, unmanageable kid. I could choose to not respond as their labels tried to define me. I could choose to redefine my life by my actions. I could choose to take control of my school life and not let labels control me. By making the right choices, I set myself free from the cube.

When I walked back into the class where kids were smiling and talking to each other, a surge of expectancy washed over me. I could make this a new day for Louie. I had learned to hate the cube and the isolation, but I also didn't realize how much the cube robbed me. There in the cube, I was the teacher, the student, and the guide. I was alone to navigate the seas of my own learning. There were things I'm sure I should have learned in fourth and most of fifth grade that I have never fully received. I was still in special education, getting help in reading and math. I was still dealing with anger, but nothing like the blowups of earlier years. Somehow, in the midst of it all, I was resilient enough to gather what I could and do my best in spite of the disadvantages I'd had to face.

By the end of sixth grade, I realized that if I was going to ever make it out of the South Side of Waukegan, I'd better stay out of the cube, and away from anything that would lead me in that direction. If I wanted to follow my friends to junior high, I needed to keep my anger under control. That's where friends like Rodney and Dax really helped. They never wanted to be "bad" guys like other kids in the neighborhood. They weren't into breaking into houses or trying to be "runners" for the gangs, like some of my other classmates who, like me, needed fast money when there was no food in the house.

Looking back now, I grew up in that cube. I put aside many of the daydreams that someone would rescue me from my anger and from poverty. By the time I was ten, I'd celebrated my last Christmas with my family, and we never put up another family tree after that. We were poor. We had no hope, and in our family, Christmas was just another day in December with nothing to celebrate.

I can remember walking home from school, cutting through alleys with Gerald, looking for bottles to return so that by the weekend I'd have enough money to ride my bike up to Belvidere mall with Rodney and the guys to play games at the arcade and eat at the Yankee Doodle Dandy Restaurant.

 Rodney and the guys didn't have to plan ahead like me. They could run in their house at a moment's notice and ask their mom or dad for a few dollars, but I had to earn and save money to join them. The pressure of earning money and planning ahead made me different. This difference didn't bother me.

I saved my money through the week from my newspaper route because I knew that Dad didn't have any money and mom's money went to keeping the rapidly deteriorating house from completely falling apart and taking care of herself during extended "bingo vacations."

Going to the Yankee Doodle Dandy was a treat. For me, I loved the idea of paying to go to the arcade and eat out with my friends. For that moment, I was a man, taking care of myself. I liked the feeling of money in my pocket even though I didn't have enough to do everything I wanted. I had enough to keep me from begging fries off a friend's plate or being left out of the fun altogether. However, I never had enough to by the Yankee Doodle Special— hamburger, fries, and a coke all for three dollars. After getting coins for the arcade, I'd only have enough to choose two out of the three options because I'd have to save at least a dollar to do my laundry. I'd have a hamburger and fries, or hamburger and a Coke—never all three. That was the thing about being poor, even though you may have more than others, there is never enough to completely satisfy the ache of not being able to get what you really want. Gerald was left out on days like this because he was worse off than I was, and there was no way he could get that far from the house, leaving his mom alone and defenseless all day with Big J.

After those days roaming through Belvidere Mall, with lunch at Yankee Doodle Dandy, we'd ride like maniacs dodging in and out of traffic on Belvidere Road, racing back to the South Side to familiar ground before dark.

I came in late one evening, and I could tell something was strange by the time I put my bike in the garage and opened the back door to the kitchen. Every light in the house was on and my mom and dad were yelling in the front room. I walked past my sister's door, and she was sitting on the edge of her bed with her tear-stained face in her hands. I got scared for a moment because my brother was the only one I hadn't seen or heard.

I wondered if he'd been hurt or shot like Skeezie; I quickly ran to the front room, ready to hear the worst, when I saw my brother sitting on the couch, lost in watching TV. Mom was yelling, "Pregnant! I can't believe she's pregnant!" Dad was standing up, breathing heavy and trying to tell Mom to calm down. Suddenly they both noticed me standing there. Like a plea for help, Dad looked at me, and I ran to the kitchen to grab his medicine and a glass of water. By the time I returned, Dad was sitting in his regular chair, breathing easier now, and Mom stood at the front door staring out into the yard.

Mumbling under her breath, "I knew this would happen, she never listens to me. I knew this would happen; what are we going to do?" Then she fell silent. My dad, finally composed, said with a voice stronger than I had heard in years, "We will do what we need to do. We will take care of our child, and we will take care of our grandchild." That is how my niece Elizabeth came to grow up with me.

By the time she was born, my brother and sister had moved out, and I had a new little sister. Dad came alive as he doted on her as he had once doted on me, and he became the one to raise Elizabeth. For the most part it was me,

Dad, and Elizabeth at home now. This new baby brought a new joy into our lives to interrupt the pain that seemed to so often plague it.

Chapter 10

THE PRAYER

*Sometimes the very thing you lack can be the thing that
leads you to your salvation. "You guys want to go eat pizza
and play some basketball?" The difference maker…*

I N MIDDLE SCHOOL, life was about baseball. Everything I did was to
ensure that I'd have enough to register for the league, buy my cleats, and
eat with the guys after the game. I'd get up early in the morning to grab
my bike and do the paper route that led me to large houses that extended
beyond the boundaries of the South Side and race back in time to get ready
for school. When we weren't playing baseball, guys from the neighborhood
would gather at King Park to play basketball and hang out.

In those days, I wasn't home much. Mom was still waiting tables down in
the rich neighborhoods, "down the North Shore Chicago Metra rail line" in
wealthy cities like Glencoe and Highland Park, but I hadn't seen any money
from my mom or dad in a couple of years. As a matter of fact, I had been
taking care of myself since I was ten years old. I thought back to the start of
the school year, when I took the thirty dollars I earned from cutting grass to
register myself for school.

When the secretary asked where my parents were, I lied and said that
they were at work. In reality, they had no idea where I was, and they hadn't
noticed that they needed to register me for school that day. I thought of how
many times I walked around doing my own school shopping at Lakehurst
Shopping Mall, trying to find the best way to spend the seventy dollars I had
managed to save from a summer of tossing newspapers, collecting bottles,
and doing odd jobs. I was on my own and 832 McAllister was the place
where my family lived, though I felt homeless and orphaned already.

One lazy afternoon after a full day at school, my friends and I were
arguing about whether we were going to spend the afternoon playing Strike
Out or basketball. As we stood on the corner of 9th and McAllister, a young
White woman drove up in a gray van, and hopped out with a warm smile,
"You guys want to go eat pizza and play some basketball?" I was stunned, so
I didn't say anything, but the other guys seemed to know who she was and
were already piling into the van.

I turned to my friend George, "Who's she?"

He said, "Louie, that's Holly. She's cool. Come on, let's go!" I agreed to follow George and the guys and couldn't help getting excited about the unexpected opportunity to have pizza. For a poor kid, there's never enough food, so any chance to eat was a chance to feel good, even if you didn't know the hand that fed you.

When we arrived at the South Side Waukegan YMCA (which was outside of our comfort zone because we knew that kids from our neighborhood weren't welcome in that part of town) Holly didn't have a care in the world. "Come on guys, I've already paid for the gym. It's all yours!" With slight reluctance, we jumped out of the van and ran into the building where Holly greeted the clerk sitting at the desk, "This is my group! We'll be eating here later too." The additional reminder about pizza was all I needed to hear to dismiss any fear and focus on having fun with friends.

I didn't know Holly too well, but if she wanted to
talk to me more about God, I sure didn't mind
having the talk while eating a slice of pizza!

After about an hour of basketball, Holly called us over to one of the side rooms off the gymnasium. She had laid out three or more steaming pizzas that drew us to the front of the room like a magnet. We started to reach for a slice, but she said, "Wait, hold on a minute. I've got to tell you something first." We all groaned and took a seat as she turned to the chalkboard and wrote the word, "JESUS." I'd never seen that word before, and I wondered what it had to do with basketball and pizza.

Holly explained that God loved each one of us. He wanted us to love Him too and live for Him. But God knew that we had a problem called sin, and so He sent His Son Jesus to take away our sin. I was pretty confused at that point. Even though I had been to family nights with Bible reading with Dax a few times, I had only been to a church once or twice, and I knew there was a God. I was shocked to find out God had a Son, and His Son's name was Jesus. I don't remember much of what else she said, but after a few moments, she said a quick prayer and said, "OK, you guys can eat!" That was all I needed to hear. I'd figure this God and Jesus stuff out later. I didn't know Holly too well, but if she wanted to talk to me more about God, I sure didn't mind having the talk while eating a slice of pizza!

Through the fall, Holly came around and talked to some of the guys. I never really got to know her that well, but for guys like George, she went to their houses and talked to them about school and family. I didn't have anyone that interested in me, and I was used to it being that way. The last time I saw Holly was around Thanksgiving that year. The weather was getting cold earlier than usual that November, and I saw the guys waiting on the corner as I was on my way to grab some food from the McAllister Grocery since we didn't have anything to eat at home. I stopped to talk to the guys: "Where are you guys going?"

"We're going with Holly to a retreat and to have Thanksgiving dinner," said George.

"Wow, Thanksgiving dinner. Can I go?"

"Yeah," said George, "Holly said anybody can go." I was excited! Thanksgiving dinner—what a treat! I was glad to save the money I had in my pocket in exchange for a great dinner that I hoped included turkey, potatoes, and gravy.

After a few minutes of excited waiting, Holly pulled up in her gray van, and we piled inside. "Hey, Louie, good to see you. Glad you're joining us..." I found a seat far in the back with George as we started on a long ride twenty-five miles away from Waukegan to the western suburb of Wheeling, Illinois. I had never been to Wheeling before, and I didn't know what a retreat was, but the promise of a Thanksgiving dinner was enough to quiet any concerns. Things only got better as we pulled in front of a large building that looked like a large house or community center. We walked inside, and the aroma of roasted turkey, pumpkin pie, mashed potatoes, and gravy poured from every room. Several adults welcomed us and led us to beautifully decorated tables filled with pumpkins and Thanksgiving decorations. All of the guys were feeling what I was feeling. Whatever we were going to experience that day, it was something we had never experienced in our neighborhood on the South Side. I sensed the excitement in the room as the program began and when we all grabbed hands before a man in the front began to pray over the meal. I don't remember what he prayed, but I do remember feeling very special and very safe, standing there holding the hands of my friends. It wasn't a feeling I had felt often, but I was thankful, and I wondered if feelings like that would ever come to stay.

Holly wasn't lying when she told us about the Thanksgiving meal. I couldn't stop smiling at the sight of my plate filled with turkey, corn, green beans, and mashed potatoes covered in gravy. This was the best meal I'd had in a long time, and it didn't matter that a bunch of people I didn't know prepared the meal. It also didn't matter that I was far from home and even my parents didn't know where I was. All that mattered was that moment of enjoying a meal with my friends. As we wrapped up our meal, the man in the front called for our attention and introduced a singing group called the Lumpkin Family Singers. They were a group of four men, a father and his three teenage sons. I was just about ready to tune them out when the music began, and the oldest boy began to sing while his father and other brothers played the drums, guitar, and piano. At one point in the song, the guy on the guitar began to rap, and from that moment I was hooked. I had never heard anything like that before, and I was excited to hear more. In their forty-five minute music set, I watched the three sons go from one instrument to another, taking turns with their dad, singing and rapping.

I'd never been to a professional concert, but I imagined that they were as good as any group that came on the radio. When the concert was finally over, the dad came to the front and explained that they had a tape of their music on sale for five dollars for anyone who was interested. I fingered the three dollars in my pocket that I had planned to use for my dinner that night. And like usual, I didn't have enough. But I wanted that tape! I went cautiously up to the tape table and told the oldest son how much I enjoyed their music. I said, "I don't have five dollars, but I'd sure like to have that tape your dad talked about." His dad must have heard me and turned with a smile, "Look, I'll make you a deal, we'll give you the tape today, and when you get five dollars, send it to the address right here on the bottom." I was blown away! "Thanks, I will." I grabbed the tape and joined my friends back at the table where everyone was eating pumpkin pie for dessert. I got my dessert and sat back with a smile on my face. Even before tasting the pumpkin pie, my heart was satisfied—filled with good things and hopes that things for me would continue to get better.

...I heard the lyrics about letting Jesus into my life ... I knelt at the foot of my bed and read the prayer exactly as it was written on the little tract inside the cassette ... I couldn't save myself, but Jesus could save me.

Within a few days after we left the retreat, I read the little tract that was inside the Lumpkin Family Singers' cassette tape and listened to the music over and over. Every song spoke directly to me, and I couldn't escape the feeling I got whenever I thought too long about God wanting to do something special with my life. Though Gerald didn't go to the retreat, I tried to explain the meal and the experience with God to him, but he didn't really care or understand. Even my friends didn't want to talk about the trip to Wheeling or the Lumpkin Family Singers, but instead wanted to talk about more interesting things, such as sports and how much fun we were planning to have over the Christmas break. I was a little disappointed that no one else cared about the retreat or the singers. No one had even gotten the tape other than me. So there I was, alone on a Saturday afternoon in my bedroom at the back of the house, not too long before Christmas. I played the tape again and as I heard the lyrics about letting Jesus into my life, it was different. I was overwhelmed. I felt emotional. I knelt at the foot of my bed and read the prayer exactly as it was written on the little tract inside the cassette. The prayer said that I knew I was a sinner, and that I needed a Savior. I couldn't save myself, but Jesus could save me. I read that if I prayed, Jesus would come into my heart, and He would change me forever. In a moment filled with a kind of stillness I can't fully explain, I gave my life to Jesus.

I was twelve years old, and my life changed that day. My heart came alive with hope and faith. I wanted to go to church. I wanted to learn more about God. I wanted to chase after this God that loved me so much that He'd send His Son to die. However, there was no church to go to and no one to tell. My friends and family had made it clear that they weren't interested. After a few moments, I smiled, wiped my eyes, put on my winter jacket, gloves, and hat, and went outside to play.

Chapter 11

BROKEN DREAM

Order is safe. Discipline is good. As independent as I was, I never imagined I'd love being a soldier.

AYS OF MIDDLE school hurried by as if time couldn't wait for me to get older. Before we knew it, our eighth grade class was taking tours around Waukegan West High School and planning for the big leap into high school with the older kids.

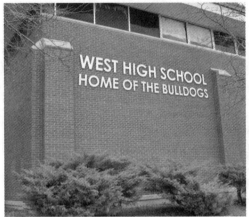

Thankfully, I hadn't gotten into much trouble at school that year, and even though I was still in special education, I was doing well in my classes. I also had the benefit of having older friends like Rodney, who was already a junior, and Dax, who was a freshmen. My friends in high school could show me the ropes without me unintentionally making a fool of myself. Even though I wasn't as fast as Rodney or as strong as Dax, I'd been playing baseball for years and chances were pretty good that I could make the varsity team.

While school was coming in to focus, things at home were worse than ever. Mom went away less, but our relationship had disintegrated into merely acknowledging one another like two ships passing in the night. My niece was getting bigger now and her little chubby fingers were getting into everything faster than my dad's hands could keep up with her. It was funny sometimes to watch them. I wondered at times who was taking care of whom. Because my niece was there, my sister had moved back in, and my brother sometimes found himself sacked out on the couch although both he and my sister had long given up the idea of going to school.

Mom was still working down the line in diners along the Chicago Metra

Train route, and she'd given me the lead on a grocery store job I worked on weekends to help pay for my clothes and food. By the time I began high school, the city of Waukegan required us to abandon our house on McAllister because of the dilapidated condition and the infestation of roaches that made it unfit for people to live in. I'd long since known that we would lose the house to neglect. The disintegration of a once beautiful, well-kept home was a mirror image of the breakdown of our family relationships. The erosion of stability in my home began so many years ago when I had to get a job to buy my own food at thirteen years old.

Too many mornings, poverty forced me to ignore the signs of the pests, to do my best to flick them out of my cereal as I grabbed a quick meal before heading out for my paper route or for school. It had been years since I had even let any friends come near our house, and for those who didn't know where I lived, I'd pretend to live at a nice, big, white house a few blocks over. When they would offer me a ride home after baseball games, I'd walk toward the door of that big white house, hoping that the owners would never peek outside and wonder why some Puerto Rican kid was walking up their drive. Then I'd turn and head around to the back of the house, pretending that I would enter the house by the back door. My friends never knew that I'd hide and run the familiar path through the alleys to the house where I really lived—a place falling apart, too broken to repair.

We quietly moved from McAllister Street to an apartment on the West Side, close enough for me to be near friends, but far enough from the constant reminder of the home we lost. I was almost thankful for the change, for the separation from the memories of the family that fell apart behind those weakened walls. In our new place, it was the six of us, Mom and Dad in one room, my sister and niece in another, and me and my brother with the smallest room in the back. I wasn't home much between school, baseball, and working two part-time jobs: one at the Jewel Osco grocery store and the other as a waiter at the kid-friendly restaurant, Chuck E. Cheese. In tenth grade however, I discovered ROTC, and it was there I discovered myself.

ROTC, or Reserve Officers Training Corps, was a big deal at Waukegan West High School. I watched the ROTC students my entire freshman year, impressed by their uniforms and intrigued by the way that they were entrusted with important tasks like carrying the flag during school assemblies and football games. When I met with my counselor to select courses for tenth grade, I knew I wanted to give ROTC a try. From the very first day, I loved it. I liked how everything was detailed and orderly and easily explained in the handbook that our teacher gave us on the second day of class. I felt proud when I realized that I was learning the same truths and principles that my dad must have heard when he joined the army after leaving Puerto Rico. There was something safe about ROTC. I found comfort in knowing what was expected of me, and then being given opportunities to show what I could do. I quickly found out that in spite of the chaos I'd grown up in, I thrived on order, on discipline, and on routine.

My ROTC teacher must have noticed it too, as I quickly began to lead my peers although some of them had been in ROTC a year before me. One of the greatest things about ROTC was the chance I had to spend time with Gerald. Changes and challenges in our lives had limited the time we spent together, so we were glad to be in the same ROTC class that fall.

I was becoming a soldier and that was comfortable for me. I'd discovered a key to survival. If I could set up my life in a series of orderly and predictable steps, then the pain, the rage, the frustration, and the chaos of poverty wasn't so acute. ROTC taught me that I could control my future.

I also knew pretty well by then that I couldn't control my family. I couldn't control my dad's illness or my mom's absences. I couldn't control the way that simple conversations between my sister, my brother, and me always ended in shouting matches. I couldn't control the dull ache that overcame me in the night sometimes, when our refrigerator was empty, my money was gone, and my father sent me to my friend's houses to eat. So much was beyond me, but baseball and ROTC were my mainstays. I was doing well in school, on the honor roll every semester and getting help in special education resource rooms with certain classes. I'd long since learned that special education didn't have to limit me. I had fought so many battles that I didn't have time or energy left to fight the labels that had been following me since kindergarten.

By 1988, I was in my junior year of high school, and things were going along well. I had become one of the three best players on the baseball team. Although my friends Rodney and Dax had graduated, I was thankful for who they were in my life. Even though I was pretty independent and focused, I know their example had a lot to do with the fact that I didn't waste my high school years partying, drinking, and chasing girls. I had spent so many years hanging out at their homes that I was impacted by their parents in ways that I never knew I needed. I can remember thinking about how I wanted to be a hard worker like Rodney's dad, and a compassionate father like Dax's dad. Rodney and Dax were great athletes with colleges knocking on their doors, and I wondered what it felt like to be wanted in such a way that would make a coach that barely knew you want to drive hours to see you play. I'd personally gotten some calls from a couple of colleges, one in Mississippi and the other a junior college in Illinois. I hadn't made any decisions yet, but it felt good to know I had options.

Besides attending school, I was on a good regimen of working about twenty hours a week to earn enough money to buy my clothes, food, and personal items. The more independent I became, the more frequently my parents looked to me to pick up a gallon of milk or to pay for a utility bill. I didn't resent it at the time, but deep down I knew that we had it backwards, and they should have been able to provide for me.

Sometime after my sixteenth birthday, I began to look past my family and see what kind of future was out there beyond the South Side for me. I didn't know how to get out, but I knew that I had to. I remember waking up early one morning to get dressed for work. In that moment of time, between being asleep and fully awake, as I lay in bed, the same feeling that I'd had years ago when I was fixing my bike in my garage came over me again. It was familiar, but not scary. As I lay there with my eyes shut, I didn't see anything this time, but it was like there was a soothingly familiar voice that spoke to my heart and said, "Louie, I'm going to do something very special in your life."

That moment was over almost as suddenly as it came. Moments like that kept the chaos of my waking hours at bay. My mom and sister still had shouting matches, and my brother and I barely spoke. But I didn't fight those battles anymore; I gave my family what I could and directed my frustrations and unanswered questions into baseball. In March of my senior year, everything fell apart.

There were scouts at the baseball game, and I knew baseball was my ticket out of the South Side. Tonight I was determined to stand out among my teammates to get the attention of those college baseball scouts. I ran to steal second base without sliding to impress those scouts watching me. The base was a hard rubbery square instead of the usual firm foam square. Rather than cushioning my foot, I bounced and heard a crack. A band of pain instantly circled my ankle. I couldn't move my ankle as I fell down in front of the crowd roaring my name.

I vaguely remember my coach calling for a time out. Then a medic and several people with a stretcher ran towards me. I was clutching my ankle, moaning because the pain seemed to take over my whole body. "Louie, we're going to take care of you," Coach said. "Relax, breathe." I gulped in the air as I held onto my Coach's neck. He pulled me up, and I hobbled off the field.

I was devastated. The hopes for my future slipped through my fingers because, without baseball, I was lost. As I rode with one of the assistant coaches to be checked out at Victory Memorial Hospital, I thought about what an injury meant for my chances of getting a baseball scholarship. After being settled in the emergency room, the nurse asked me for my phone number so that they could call my dad and ask him to come get me.

I knew something that she didn't know. My dad was too weak and too fragile to come all the way down to the hospital on his own. He had long since given up taking trips outside of the house because the polluted air was too much for his weakened lungs to handle. I knew he couldn't come, and I also knew that my mom wouldn't be around until much later that night when she finished her shift at the diner and made her way home on the evening train. There was no one to call, and everyone was distressed about that fact except me.

I finally convinced my coach that I'd be all right if he'd just give me a ride home. He consented, and I hobbled my way out to his car, trying to carefully balance myself on one leg and a new set of crutches. My coach only agreed to drop me off in peace after I safely made it in the house, and he confirmed I was OK. I agreed, and we made our way to my apartment on Waukegan's west side. He pulled right in front and came around to help me get out of the car without further injury to myself. "OK, Louie, I'm going to be right here and once you're in and you're ok, just wave to me from the door, and I'll be on my way."

"No problem, Coach, thanks again," I said as I turned to head toward the apartment building.

When I got to the door, I found it unlocked, which was strange, even though Dad was always home. I nudged the door open and became speechless as I looked inside. Everything was gone.

Chapter 12

ABANDONED

*When the future comes early, you can hold on to the
past and let the hurt and bitterness chain you, or
embrace the future and push the door open.*

ASIDE FROM A banged up kitchen table, a broken chair, and some trash in the kitchen, everything was gone. I was still trying to wrap my mind around what was going on when I found the note, scrawled in my mom's familiar handwriting: "Go Live with Your Friends." I felt as if someone sucked the air out of me. Tears stung the back of my eyes as the weight of what was happening came crashing down around me. With my voice caught in my throat, I gingerly made my way to every room, saving mine for last. Everything was gone, and my room alone was as I had left it earlier that morning except for the items that belonged to my brother. There was no more explanation and no more words. I was alone. The walls of our house had fallen down, and the weight seemed to bury me.

My coach must have thought that something was wrong because I never came back to the door to let him know everything was OK. I don't know what I would have done or said had I remembered that he was out there waiting. After a few moments, he was at the door calling my name. I didn't have words yet to answer; I was too choked up with anger, rage, and fear of the unknown. He eventually made his way to my room where he found me clutching my mother's hand-scrawled note. When he saw my face, the bewilderment etched on his was erased as he realized what I knew. My family had left me.

My coach quietly sat down next to me and asked the question that I had been silently rolling through my mind, "Where will you go?" I turned to him, not looking for pity or explanation, "I don't know, but I can't stay here anymore." I stood up and slowly began to gather my things, placing what I could in laundry baskets, crates, and pillowcases. There wasn't a lot, mainly because I'd left so much behind in our broken home on McAllister street, and because I spent more money on trying to eat than on clothes and shoes. After about forty-five minutes, we loaded my coach's car, and I had finally told him about one place I could go, even if only for one night.

"Dax's house, take me to Dax's house," I said. Even though Dax had gone away to college at Creighton University, I had shared enough meals with his family to at least hope that they could help me figure out what to do next. Maybe I was naïve, or too overwhelmed to think rationally, but inside I pinned all my hope on the Jones family during the short ride to their bungalow. My coach parked in front of the house, and when I went to turn the door handle, he reached out his arm to stop me. "No, stay here, I'll be right back." I guess he wanted to spare me the embarrassment of what might happen if the Joneses said no, and I didn't have the strength to insist that I go to the door myself to plead my case. I rolled down the window and sat there for almost an hour, not worried about what the Jones family would say, but vacillating between anger, embarrassment, hurt, and shame that my entire family had left me. I wanted to lash out, to make them feel the pain they had inflicted on me. I wanted to know why. What had I done wrong; how long had they plotted to slip away without me in their lives? These questions remained unanswered as Chuck came to the car and gently opened the door. "Come on, Louie, let's go have a talk," Chuck beckoned me to come inside. Something about his tone of voice let me know that he wasn't blaming me for the situation I had awkwardly placed his family in. I slid out of the car, now noticing a significant throb in my ankle, and slowly hopped my way to the door. Once inside, Kim, Dax's mom, looked strained as I walked into the room. I could hear Dax's little brothers, Jordan and Clay, playing in the back room, while Bethany practiced her flute behind a closed bedroom door. "Louie, sit down over here. I'm so sorry..." Kim began, but being choked up with emotion, she looked to Chuck for help. Her tears let me know that things might not work out as well as I had hoped, but Chuck quickly spoke up. "Louie, we know that this isn't your fault, and it definitely isn't the best situation that you find yourself in, but there is a solution here. God always has a way of working everything out for our good. Now, you know Dax is gone off to school, but we've shared enough ball games and meals with you, Louie, to know that you're a good kid. I haven't talked to your folks, and I don't know all of what's going on, but I do know that we can make room for you here. Me and Kim and the kids, we're family, and if you're going to be here, you'll be a part of our family. You'll do what we do, follow our rules, eat with us, and you'll have a place here for as long as you need it."

The room grew silent as the weight of all that Chuck said slowly sank in. I didn't know how to feel. Tenderly accepted and brutally rejected in the space of the same day. I was numb. All I could say in that moment was "thank you." The rest of their conversation was a blur as I tried to comprehend that

I wouldn't be spending the night on the street and that the vortex of this terrible day might finally be coming to an end. After a few minutes, my coach and Chuck grabbed my few items from the car, and Kim stood up to finish preparing dinner. I remember sitting there wondering how life could go on like normal while my world was crashing in around me. I was sixteen years old, my baseball dreams were destroyed, my ankle broken, and everything I owned was lined up neatly along the wall in a house that wasn't mine. I emerged from the fog long enough to thank my coach and to ask him not to tell anyone what had happened to me. My coach responded, "Don't worry, Louie, I'm glad I was here for you today." I nodded as I turned away, not wanting to acknowledge the tears that pressed behind my eyes.

I sat down on the couch and almost immediately fell asleep. I don't know if it was the stress of the day that finally wore me out, but I remember waking up a few hours later with a blanket gently laid across me and the faint glow of light coming from the kitchen. It was dark outside, and the house was quiet as if everyone was asleep. I rubbed my eyes wondering for a moment where I was and what time it was, and then at once I remembered. Fully awake now, I made a move to get up and clumsily knocked my bandaged foot against the coffee table. Chuck and Kim must have heard me as they both came into the living room.

Kim began, "Louie, there's some dinner on the stove if you're hungry. You'll be staying in Bethany's room, and there's towels in the bathroom when you're ready." For a moment, I just stared at her. I couldn't believe that she was being so kind to me. I searched her eyes first, then those of her husband, and the question that filled my mind was *why*? Not *why did they leave*? or *why did this happen*? but *why would you be so nice and do this for me when you don't have to*? Chuck seemed to understand almost immediately. He told me, "Louie, we are a Christian family. Above everything we do, that's who we are. It's our Christian duty to open our home, and our lives, to you in your time of need."

Although I didn't understand much about what being a Christian meant, beyond the experience I'd had with God in the back bedroom of my house on McAllister Street, I was thankful that they seemed to know more, and do more for me, because of it. By the time I went to bed that night after a quiet dinner and hot shower, I at least had a hope that everything would eventually be all right.

Two weeks later as we were eating dinner, my mom came knocking on the door. I could see her red hair through the screen door. Kim didn't want to answer the door. She kept setting the table. I stood up and opened the door. "Hi, Mom," I said casually, as if the empty apartment and the cruel note she left behind never happened.

"Hi, Louie, how are you?" she asked as she came inside the house.

"I'm good, Mom. What's going on?"

She clutched her purse closely to her side and said, "Louie, I need forty dollars. The baby needs milk." She didn't explain her sudden disappearance a few weeks ago, and the fury that I felt that night was gone. Instead, I looked at a woman who was a shadow of her former days as a stunning beauty that would stop traffic. There were lines around her eyes and mouth. Traces of cigarette ashes were under her fingernails. "OK, Mom, wait here."

I went into my bedroom and pulled out my wallet. I'd just been paid, and I had a few hundred dollars that I was saving for college. The Joneses fed me, and I was frugal with my money. I pulled out two twenty dollar bills. "Here, Mom; here's forty dollars." She took the money and carefully put them in her frayed wallet. "Well, you look like you're doing good," she said glancing over to Kim and Chuck. Kim stared away. "I gotta go, Louie," she hugged me. "Thank you for the money."

I sighed. "Yeah, tell Dad hi," I said. I worried about my dad because I was the one that made sure he got his medications when he was supposed to take them.

"Louie, how could you give her money?" Kim asked as she watched Mom get into the car parked in front of the house. I looked down at the wood floor. I knew Kim couldn't understand my mom or why she left me, but for some reason I understood her life, even though she never confided in me but talked to my older brother. "She doesn't know any better," I said. "It's not her fault." Kim's hazel eyes widened in amazement.

How could she understand a woman who had to hustle to feed three kids—a woman who scratched the underbelly of life to survive?

Chapter 13

BASEBALL DREAM

Doors open and others close. I've learned enough to know that it's not important to do the opening or the closing. The important thing is that when doors open, I've got to have the courage to walk through them.

I LIVED WITH THE Jones family through the rest of my senior year and celebrated my graduation in June of 1989. I was the only one of my mother's three children to graduate. I'd done something to be proud of, and I knew the price that I'd paid to put on my cap and gown that warm spring day. My ankle had healed, and in spite of my recent injury, I'd been recruited by Kishwaukee Community College, the number one baseball junior college in the country.

Kishwaukee Community College is located about two hours west of Chicago in a small suburban town, Malta, in western Illinois. Though I'm sure people go to college for lots of different reasons, I went to college to get as far from Waukegan as I could and to play baseball. So, with hundreds of other freshmen, I arrived on campus that fall not really knowing what to expect next. I loved baseball, and I loved being on the team. Being a part of sports was relaxing for me because I didn't mind working hard, and there was nothing like the excitement of a ball game with the wind in your face and the entire team pulling together for a big win.

The first few days after arriving on campus were good. Everyone was excited about the prospect of a new year, and it was refreshing, yet scary, to finally be out of Waukegan. I had talked to my family and the Joneses once or twice, but in spite of the bustling college crowd, I was at college alone and on my own. The money I had saved from working at the grocery store through the summer didn't last long as I struggled to buy books, food, and the few items I needed for my dormitory room. Classes were different too. Instead of the familiar halls of Waukegan West High School, I had to cross an expansive campus as I ran into teachers who were more concerned with their teaching than with what we were actually learning.

The only place where I was confident was on the baseball field. I was on a partial scholarship for baseball, and that gave me enough positive self-esteem to know that for baseball, at least, they had found a value in me. I'd gone to the Student Center to get help with my writing for Freshmen Composition Class and was working regularly with a girl named Angela. She was different from anyone who had ever helped me. I was nervous for her to see my work—afraid that she'd ridicule me. I was surprised to hear her say, "Louie, you know what you're doing. Your ideas are good. You just have to believe in yourself. I can help you with spelling and all the other stuff, but your ideas are strong. You may not believe me, but you're really smart."

Wow, I wasn't expecting that. I didn't know what to do at first. Her words began to stack up against the twelve years I'd spent in special education with teachers and principals and classmates telling me how dumb I was. Her words were like water to refresh the hope that had been stolen away by too much strain and not enough good days. I decided to take a leap and believe her. I decided to believe what the voice had told me about having a special plan for my life. I decided to believe, and for the first time, I looked at my own work—thoughts from my own mind and writings from my own hand—and I was not ashamed. Angela was excited, too, when I got my essay back from my teacher with a "B" at the top with bold red letters. It was a hard-earned grade, but what I discovered about myself was much more valuable.

As the semester went on, the costs of laundry and food and incidentals quickly added up. When there is no one to send care packages from home or to add money to my student account, things got bad fast. By mid-semester, I withdrew from classes to work to pay for food. I returned to the South Side of Waukegan frustrated and in defeat. This time though, I didn't go back to my parent's home or the Jones'. Chuck had worked out a great deal for me by connecting me with a man at his church who left his apartment empty during the week as he attended classes and worked in the city only to return home on weekends. I was able to live at the apartment as long as I needed to, just as long as I kept the place clean. That was easy enough for me, and I spent most of my time working and trying to figure out what to do next.

Some afternoons, I'd go by and visit with the Jones family, and on one occasion, Chuck asked me to join him at a local restaurant for breakfast the next morning so that we could talk. After breakfast, Chuck was serious as he sat up in his chair and leaned toward the table. He took out a pen and paper and began to write. "Louie," he said, "you need a place to live. You need a place to eat. You need someone to take care of you. And you need to learn a trade. Louie, I think you need to consider going into the military."

At first, I was stunned. No, absolutely not. I couldn't go into the military. I was supposed to play baseball. No matter how hungry I'd been the previous semester, no matter how hard it was and how poor I was, I had to figure out a way to get to some college where I could live and play baseball. In the back of my mind, I knew that I wanted to go and do what Dax was doing. He was playing baseball, and he was in college, but I didn't have that reality. I didn't have parents. Chuck reminded me of how well I had done in ROTC in high school and how much I seemed to enjoy learning about the military. We talked a little while longer about what joining the military could mean for me. Chuck jolted me into reality and caused me to see that the military could do all the things for me that I could not do for myself. When I realized the truth of his words, I thought, *The military . . . they will take care of me.* For the first time in my life, I thought, *Yes, I won't have to scratch to survive— I'll be taken care of.*

By the next week, I was in the recruiters' office making plans to take the military entrance exam and pack my things for boot camp. I left in March of 1990, and my whole world changed. I was eighteen years old, and that's when my life began.

Chapter 14

FIRST FLIGHT—NO MORE CHAOS

You don't know who you can really be sometimes unless you give yourself a fresh start. A new start helps to discover the new you.

MY LIFE BEGAN at age eighteen with my first flight. The army recruiter picked me up at five o'clock that morning, and I boarded a plane at Chicago's O'Hare airport for the first leg of my journey toward Fort Sill, Oklahoma. I was scheduled to fly to St. Louis, Missouri, first before connecting with a flight that would take me on to Oklahoma. I'd never flown before, and I can't fully describe the jumble of emotions that bombarded me as I thanked my recruiter and held my boarding pass firmly in my hand. I had a couple of hours to wait before my flight left, and I spent the time thinking about what lay ahead and all the things I was glad to leave behind. By 7:00 a.m., we were in the air, and I was on my way, seeing the world from a whole new perspective and hoping that my view above the clouds was only a hint of the good things to come. Breathing in deeply, I began to release fear and breathe in hope for a new day.

I arrived in St. Louis and grabbed a bite to eat. I had already been forewarned about a long layover, so I wandered the airport before taking my place at my assigned gate later that day. My adventure, for once, wasn't hindered by my poverty or my past. I was being reborn right before my eyes, and there was nothing and no one to stop me. It was late when my flight to Oklahoma was finally called. I knew I'd have to ride a bus to the base for a while even after landing at the airport, but Fort Sill would be my new home, and I hoped it was worth the wait. When I finally got on the plane in St. Louis, something broke in me, and I cried. It was as if the tears from a million disappointments spilled out of me at once. I didn't cry for my mother or my father. I didn't cry because of broken relationships with my sister or my brother. For once, without apology, I cried for me. It was bittersweet. It was sweet because I was leaving. It was bitter because of the pain of thinking "Forget you all. I'll show you." I wiped my face unashamed and in my heart I knew, "I'm never going back. Never."

I finally arrived at the base in Fort Sill, Oklahoma, around eight o'clock that evening. I couldn't see anything in the dark on the ride in from the airport, and the other soldiers and I filed into the Army Reception Area. In the reception area, everyone was nice and welcoming. They fed us well, and I spent about four days there filling out paperwork, taking examinations, getting uniforms and schedules, and getting my hair cut. I felt like I was in heaven. There was order, structure, and plenty of food. They gave me an advance pay of two hundred dollars, and that was the most I'd had in my pocket in a long time. The army gave that money so that soldiers like me could purchase their personal items.

I had a fresh haircut, my BDUs (Battle Dress Uniform), and a dream in front of me. I was feeling good. This was a good decision. I didn't care what anyone thought. In my heart I knew, "This is good for me. I'm going to make it." I even gave up the dream of baseball. I'm not doing that, I'm doing this. Every thought in me let me know that joining the US Army was what I needed to do.

I was so thankful to be sleeping in a bed. I was going to be trained to do a job. I had a future. I had money in my pocket. The food was good. There was order. There was structure, and I loved that. I felt comfortable. Because of ROTC, I actually had a leg up on everyone else because I knew my chain of command. I knew my rank and my drill. I knew things that the other guys didn't know because they never had ROTC. I even had a little bit of rank and came in as an E-3 instead of an E-1 because of ROTC. My rank also allowed me to lead, even from the beginning.

Those of us who had ROTC experience were put in charge of a few other soldiers to help them learn the ropes of military life. My life had changed, and I was on my way.

I loved the military, and I was surprised at how quickly I felt at home. I was fed up with the instability back in Waukegan—the not knowing what I was going to do, the lack of order. Unlike many of the new recruits, basic training for me wasn't hell on earth. ROTC helped me to know what to expect so I wasn't surprised by the two-week shock phase with the drill sergeant. ROTC prepared me to be ready to take orders and to give orders. I knew the language, the culture, and the structure of the military, and I fit in like a hand in a glove. I think army life impacted me on another level because of my personal need for structure and order.

I completed basic training in Fort Sill and boarded a bus headed to advanced training. As we prepared to leave the post, I realized that I really hadn't seen anything beyond the base. We had arrived in the dark of night, and we hadn't left the post for the entire two weeks of basic training. I was excited to see where I was and to experience this new place that was so different from the South Side of Waukegan. After our basic training graduation, we left Fort Sill and rode for about twelve hours through Oklahoma and Texas. Though the ride to Fort Bliss was long, I enjoyed it because I'd never seen that part of the country before. It was amazing. There were mountains that looked nothing like anything I'd seen in the flat lands of the Midwest. It was strange, as if I was visiting another country, but I liked it. It was a great adventure and I wasn't going to look back. We arrived at Fort Bliss in El Paso, Texas, and my eyes, my heart, and my future were wide open.

Chapter 15

WARTIME

War redefines your priorities even if you're not fighting on the front. Everyone is fighting when it's wartime. No one is exempt from duty because we're all fighting a war.

ORT SILL WAS like paradise compared to the older barracks on Fort Bliss. When we pulled onto the base, I wondered if we had arrived at the right place. Fort Sill had dormitory-style housing, and Fort Bliss's housing was in World War II style barracks. The old tin buildings would be my home for the next eight weeks of Army Advanced Training. "I think we took a step down," I said under my breath to my friend next to me. "Look at these barracks, they are old!" The gray walls and tin roof didn't look like home, but this day was still one of the best days of my life because I was living it for *me*.

I had been promoted to platoon leader since I was the only one in my unit that had military experience through high school ROTC. I was in charge of my group, and everyone called me PG (Platoon Guide). I was being trained for the infantry as a gunner on the Bradley Fighting Vehicle. For the first time, I had the respect of a group of men who looked up to me. The labels that defined me for so many years—unmanageable, special education, hyper, bad—were torn off. Instead, I was responsible, respectable, and a leader.

That first weekend at Fort Bliss, my drill sergeant said my unit could go out on a weekend pass. I had been in the army for fourteen weeks and had not eaten at a McDonald's or worn civilian clothes. For the first time in my life, I had over twelve hundred dollars cash since the army paid four hundred a month. I couldn't believe that I had more money than anyone in my family. I took seven hundred dollars and jumped in a cab with a bunch of guys to go to the mall. It felt good having cash in my pocket and not having to worry about where I was going to live or eat. I had a place to go back to, transportation at my disposal, and I could buy anything I wanted. The claw of poverty that gripped my life for so many years was losing its power. In all my life, I had never experienced the amazing feeling of being secure, confident, and sure that everything was being take care of. I was enjoying the new life the army provided for me.

After eight weeks of advanced training, my commanding officer gathered us to tell us our post assignments for next year. I hadn't thought much about where I wanted to go as long as it wasn't back to Waukegan. Finally, I heard, "Reyes...Korea." I thought, *Korea...what?* Another guy and I out of the platoon were being sent to Korea. Everyone else was going to Europe or other posts in the States. I was in shock, but I was excited, too, as I prepared to leave the United States for the first time. First, however, I had to make it through the two weeks leave I was given in order to visit my family.

By September 1990, I had been in the US Army for six months. I said I would never go back to Waukegan, but by this time, I really missed my dad. I longed to hear his husky voice in person and to see his face. I had never been away from home for so long, so I hopped a plane back to Chicago. I was nineteen years old, and all of my friends were away at college.

Waukegan was quiet, and there wasn't much going on. I spent most of my two weeks with my dad, although I also spoke to the ROTC group at Waukegan West High School. My army recruiter told me that I needed to speak to the group since I was an alumni of the program. I enjoyed telling eager high school students about my adventures of going through basic training and advanced training. Most of these students were like me and had never been on a plane or out of the state. Oklahoma, Texas, and New Mexico were almost like foreign countries to them.

"I've been watching a lot of the news lately and we've gone to war." I was shocked because I hadn't heard anything during advanced training about a war.

On the last day of my two-week leave, as I said goodbye to my dad, he hugged me and said, "Louie, where you going again?"

I said, "Dad, I'm going to Korea."

He said, "I've been watching a lot of the news lately and we've gone to war." I was shocked because I hadn't heard anything during advanced training about a war. "Look at the TV, Louie," he motioned to me. There were groups of soldiers wearing muted, yellow camouflage gear, boarding planes and preparing supplies on military vehicles.

"Don't worry, Dad; that's not us," I said. "We wear green fatigues." The US had just invaded Iraq, and I didn't know that the army was being called up. The only thing I knew was that I had orders to go to Korea.

After flying from Chicago, I again had a layover in St. Louis; in the airport, I saw a sea of men and women in desert fatigues. I asked a group who they were with and where they were going. "We're with the army," one of the guys answered. "We're going to Saudi Arabia." That's when I learned that the army had desert forces. The reality of war was settling in.

I flew to Oakland from St. Louis and saw throngs of men and women in desert fatigues. Operation Desert Storm had started, and my orders were taking me to the other side of the world. I ran into my friend James at the gate who was dressed in civilian clothes. "We're going to war, Louie," he said. "Everybody is going to Saudi." I reminded James that we were going to Korea and if Saudi was in the plans, then we'd have to be ready.

We boarded a massive plane to Korea and landed at Osan Air Base in Pyeongtaek, South Korea. As I got off the plane, we walked into a hub of activity as sand-colored tanks, Humvees, and aircrafts were being shipped by massive C130 aircrafts to Saudi Arabia. My heart sank because I realized that many of those men and women that I saw in the St. Louis and Oakland airports could die in war. I wanted to weep for them, but I held myself in check. We all knew what we signed up to do when we joined the military.

New soldiers like me were picked up and taken to Camp Casey in Dongducheon, our final destination until the army told us to go somewhere else. War was taking place in the Middle East, but our job was to hold down the Demilitarized Zone. In Korea, I was surprised at how everyone looked the same. They had the same eyes, same facial shape, same nose, and same raven black hair. I had never been in a place where everyone looked the same. The months went by, and I missed home. I hardly called home because it was so expensive, and it was difficult to get access to use a land line phone.

I was one of thousands of new recruits that had never been out of the country or away from home. Our base, Camp Casey, had over 6,000 military personnel and almost everything you would want was within a five-minute drive or a bike ride. Once soldiers were off base though, we had to be careful of bars that emptied the pockets of military men. Some of my friends fell prey to pretty women who would lure them into a bar and then get them to spend money on them. Fortunately, since I wasn't a drinker, bars were not attractive to me.

On Christmas Day, I was assigned to serve guard duty in a guard tower. I had to stand in a guard shack watching the snowfall across the Dongducheon South Korea base while everyone else celebrated the holidays. It was a beautiful night, and I got emotional when I thought about how far I'd come from the South Side of Waukegan. When New Year's Eve came around, I was invited to go to a party with my platoon. I had never been to a nightclub, never drank alcohol, and never smoked a cigarette.

When we got to the club (which was actually a converted multi-purpose room with lights, a DJ, dance floor, and bar), I was ready to experience the nightlife I'd heard so much about. I walked in with my friends, and then I broke away to find a girl to dance with. The air was thick with smoke and the smell of alcohol. I wanted to have fun, but I felt uncomfortable as if I was on another planet. The smoke was stinging my eyes, and I didn't like the smell of alcohol, but I figured that I could still have fun dancing. A girl caught my eye, and as I was walking towards her, a voice spoke into my heart, "What are you doing here? You're not supposed to be in here." The voice scared me because it came from my heart with the authority of a commander. It was familiar, and I immediately knew I had to respond. And like a soldier who had been given a command, I turned around and walked out of the club.

The bus that had just brought all of us to the club was pulling away from the front of the building. With my heart racing, I ran to the bus and pounded on the door screaming to the driver to stop. He looked shocked as he opened the door for me. I couldn't tell him what was wrong, and I was the only passenger on the bus since it was so early. He took me back to the bus stop near my barracks, and as I started walking away from the bus, I noticed that a light was on in the building shaped like a half-moon hut. As I got closer, I could tell this was the base church that held services for Catholics, Koreans, Protestants, and Baptists. I heard Christian music coming from the building, and I felt compelled to go inside.

A group of men and women were standing in a half-circle, and I approached them slowly. "What are you doing?" I asked quietly.

A guy answered, "We're praying in the New Year."

"What does that mean?" I asked.

The man smiled and said, "You know, asking for God's favor and blessing on the New Year."

For the first time, I felt an overwhelming peace as I listened to these men and women talk to God like they knew Him. They prayed for healing in marriages and protection for family back home.

I almost began to weep as they prayed for the families who had lost loved ones that year and those who were unashamed to pour out their lives for God. By the time the prayer ended, God spoke to me that this was where I needed to be. I never went back to a bar or a nightclub.

Chapter 16

GOD'S CALLING

Most people have no idea what their destiny is in God. Destiny
is usually right in front of us, waiting for us to act. Our
response to God can save a life or delay Him in breaking into
another person's life because God works through people.

AFTER SPENDING A year in Korea, attending church, and getting
more familiar with God's voice, the army decided I had been there
long enough, and ordered me to go to Fort Carson Army Base in
Colorado Springs, Colorado. I had worked hard, stayed out of the bars and
clubs, and had saved enough money to buy my first car with cash. When I
walked into the dealership during my leave back in Illinois to pick up my
Cayman Green Ford Escort GT, you would have thought I was driving a
Rolls Royce. I had paid for the car through electronic payments during my
year in Korea and the sacrifice was worth it.

My relationship with
God solidified during the
year in Korea. Even though
I travelled from Illinois
across the country to my
new post in Colorado
Springs alone, I knew that
He was there with me.
There was something about
God's presence that made
the miles fade away and
caused me to be filled with
a sense of wonder and peace. I knew I was guided by someone who would
take care of me, not like the army, but someone who would help me navigate
through the thoughts and pictures that popped up in my dreams or when a
thought triggered a horrific memory from the past.

I loved Fort Carson and quickly adjusted to military life in Colorado. My
first mission was to find a church. My experience in Korea taught me the
value of finding other believers to grow in faith with and share God's Word.

On one of my days off, I drove around the city near the base and noticed a storefront mission for the homeless that was also a Pentecostal church. I was attending church and getting to know people. One day, my friend Pat Noland introduced me to an older gentleman, Alvin, who was starting a Pentecostal Holiness Church, Deliverance Tabernacle. It was exciting to meet people who were stepping out and doing things for God. Alvin gave me his Bible, and I still preach from that Bible today. Not long after meeting Alvin, and getting more excited about doing things for God, one of Pat's friends got in a motorcycle accident and Pat came to me, asking me to pray for his friend.

I was terrified, and I called Chuck for advice. "Hi, Chuck, my friend wants me to pray for his friend who was in an accident," I said. "I don't know what to say."

Chuck responded, "Louie, you can do this. Just talk to God."

I was still nervous because I didn't have a script. "What do I say?" I asked clutching my Bible.

"Just talk to God like He's a person in the room. What would you say to someone standing next to your friend who has the power to heal?" That sounded easy to do. I didn't want to be embarrassed because I had never prayed aloud like that. I had bowed my head when I was asked to in church when the pastor prayed, but other than those scant prayer experiences, I had none.

"OK, I think I can do that," I told Chuck. "I'll pretend I'm talking to you." He laughed, and I hung up the phone. I walked down the hospital hallway and Pat was standing next to his friend Guthrie's bed. Bandages covered Guthrie's leg, and an IV line was stuck into his arm. He looked exhausted.

"Guthrie, this is my friend Louie who I was telling you about," Pat said. "We go to church together." Guthrie looked at me dazed. I don't know if it was the pain medications or tiredness from the ordeal of tests and operations. I held my hand out, and he weakly shook my hand.

"Guthrie, can I pray for you?" I asked. He nodded and laid back. I don't remember the words that I said, but I remember I felt chills up and down my spine and a presence weigh on me. I don't remember what happened to Guthrie, but I remember Guthrie thanking me for praying for him, and I walked back into the hallway overcome by a presence of joy, love, and peace that wrapped around me like a blanket.

When I sat in the chair in the hallway, I felt the same presence that came to me when I was eight years old. I heard an inner voice that seemed to be quiet and shouting at the same time saying, "I'm going to use you, Louie." I heard this voice twice, and I was so overcome by this voice that seemed to call out from another world to me that I was crying.

People were walking by as I wept, and I knew then that God was calling me into the ministry. I didn't know how it was going to happen or what that meant, but I knew that God was calling me. I knew there was a destiny on my life that I couldn't accomplish on my own.

A few months later, Pat found Grace Fellowship, which is now called Church for All Nations. I'd allowed my faith to get cold, and I had quit going to Deliverance Tabernacle and started sleeping in on Sundays and going fishing. One Sunday I was still sleeping, and I heard a rap on the door. I got up and Pat was standing in the doorway. "I found us a church, Louie," Pat said. I asked Pat to wait and got ready to go to church with him.

When I walked through the doors of Grace Fellowship, it was completely opposite of any church experiences I'd had up to that point.

The church had about five hundred people, and you could feel the excitement about following God as soon as you walked through the doors. The worship team was a full band that captured me with their passionate energy. This was not a boring choir or a half-baked, one-man worship show. Their worship team included all sorts of instruments and quality vocalists. They could have passed as a professional band.

Pastor Mark Cowart's message that Sunday immediately caught my heart. I felt challenged, like I could step up in my faith and be one of the people the Bible talked about who lived in faith as a lifestyle. I instantly liked his messages and Texas-accented preaching styles. As he preached, I felt like he was telling everything about my life and my issues—even though he didn't know me—but I wasn't embarrassed. I knew that God was speaking to me through him.

One Sunday morning after attending the church for a few months, I stepped out of the service to use the restroom. I passed by the Children's Ministry classrooms, and I heard children laughing as music played in the room. Since I didn't grow up in church, naturally, I was curious about how the children's service was different from the adult's experience. I looked through the glass window on the door and was stunned by the puppet show that portrayed a Bible story and songs. I had never seen anything like it. The children were smiling and laughing at the show that had been prepared just for them. I don't know how long I stood there, but something in me had changed. I was different.

Next Sunday I left the service at the same time to see another puppet show. This week the puppets were even better as they portrayed the Bible stories and life lessons that even a little child could understand. I didn't know why I was so drawn, but there was a curiosity brewing inside of me.

After attending the church regularly for six months, a single lady in her forties, Connie Schooler, asked me to help her with the children's ministry.

I had never talked to a woman in her forties about anything personal like working for God, and I never considered working with kids in church. "You have a great smile and such positive energy," she said. "You would make a great teacher with the kids."

I said, "No thank you. I want to usher or join the choir." I was twenty years old, and the last thing I thought about when it came to ministry was working with kids.

But Connie wouldn't take my rejection. She continued to talk to me about helping her with the kids until after one service, I said, "I'll try it," just to get her off my back. I imagined myself showing Connie how I couldn't do children's ministry so I could pursue ushering or being in the choir.

Connie was so excited, she pulled my arm through the crowds to introduce me to Lisa Dubois, the Children's Ministry Director. Connie told Lisa that she noticed my energy and charisma and thought I could help Lisa. I was scared and nervous about the idea of talking to kids about God, but since it was only going to be one week, I figured I would survive.

Chapter 17

TALKING TO KIDS ABOUT GOD

*Dreams can come true that are beyond our understanding
and break the limits of our past. Your dream come
true could be as close as tomorrow with someone
who gives you a chance, or you taking a risk.*

AFTER OBSERVING AND being trained by Lisa for a few weeks in children's ministry, she mentioned that she wanted me teach the object lesson in the next class. An object lesson is a visual aid that teaches a lesson to the kids to help them understand the Bible principle that we were teaching. I was more nervous about the prospect of teaching an object lesson to the kids than when I had to deal with enemy fire in a tank. That night I practiced the object lesson over and over again. I stood in front of the mirror and checked my facial expressions because I knew I'd have to be exaggerated in my expressions and gestures in order to hold the kids' attention.

That Sunday, when I did the object lesson in front of the kids, they were electrified. I was so excited that they liked me and were listening. I realized the power of a simple object lesson in bringing God close to the heart of a child. I was addicted to the high of sharing a concept from the Word of God and seeing the light come on in their eyes as they engaged in the lesson I taught.

While the kids loved me, I was still haunted by my past. Lisa began talking to me about the possibility of being a children's pastor. I told her, "You don't understand, Lisa. I'm from a poor home in Waukegan. Everyone in Waukegan told me that I was stupid and dumb. I was in special education. I can't teach anybody." My insecurities were at an all-time high, but I couldn't escape the way I felt when I stood in front of those kids.

I was twenty years old, and I had energy to burn. Even though I was still serving in the military, I spent my free time trying to figure out how to improve the children's ministry. I spent every Saturday at the church preparing for Sunday. I tried to add something new to every Sunday children's service. I was so interested in trying to build a quality ministry for children that I enrolled in a professional clown college in Denver to learn how to be a clown. I created a new persona for ministry—Jingles the Clown was born, and the children's ministry at Grace Fellowship Church was changed forever!

In children's ministry, I could make the kids laugh or cry with an object lesson. I had no idea that this could be a gift from God because I felt so natural talking to kids about Him. The kids didn't want to leave those services, and they started telling their friends that they needed to come to church. After three months, Lisa gave me my own class.

During that time of teaching, learning, and sharing God's Word with children, I had a dream that gave me a clue to my destiny. I was sleeping in my barracks, and I had a dream that I was watching a black truck pull up into a park. The truck had a stage that folded up. I walked up to the stage, and a guy was doing a puppet show for the kids. Kids were sitting on the ground and laughing. I laughed so hard that I woke myself up.

The following week at church, Lisa and I were preparing for a children's service. I told her about the dream. "I've heard of something like that, Louie," she said. "There's a guy named Bill Wilson who does a program like that for kids. I just read about it in *Charisma* magazine." She got up, walked out of the room, and came back in holding the magazine. I opened the magazine to the story about Bill Wilson. He was sitting in front of the truck that was in my dreams with a bunch of smiling kids. I couldn't believe that Bill Wilson had the truck of my dreams. I knew that this man was somehow in my future. I pulled out the form to order the video tape about the ministry.

A few months later, Lisa shared with me that she needed more help in children's ministry. "Louie, do you mind being my right-hand man," she said. "You can sub in all the departments and be involved in the planning." I was twenty-one years old and eager to help organize and lead in any way I could.

I was also ready to leave the army. I had served my time and the army provided excellent leadership training and opportunities for growth. Pastor Mark found out that I was ready to leave the military and asked me to meet with him.

"What do you want to do, Louie?" he asked me.

I said, "I want to go back to school to learn how to be a teacher."

He smiled and responded, "Well, my wife Linda came to me and asked if you could be our children's pastor." I was flattered that his wife suggested that I step in as the children's pastor, but I had no ministry training.

"I need training because I don't know what I'm doing," I told him. "Where did you go to get training for ministry?"

He replied, "I went to Rhema Bible College."

I did a little research and found out that Rhema Bible College was hosting a Getting Acquainted Weekend. I decided on the spot to drive down to Broken Arrow, Oklahoma, to check out the Bible college. As I drove down, I remember wondering if God was going to make a way for me to attend college after my failed attempt at Kishwaukee Community College. Somehow, I knew that if God opened the door, He would provide. As I arrived on campus, I was overwhelmed. I had never seen so many Christian young adults just like me in one place. The weekend was fun; however, I knew I didn't want to attend Rhema Bible College. I didn't want to be away from my new family at Grace Fellowship Church.

Pastor Mark called me and asked what I thought of the school. "Pastor, I really don't want to be away from my family at Grace Fellowship," I said. "I had fun, but I don't want to be away from everyone here." At that point, Pastor Mark was like a father and a mentor to me. I wanted to learn more from him.

"Brother Louie, we can teach you everything here," he said. "You can learn everything you need to know about children's ministry in a local church." I accepted the position and my first job out of the military was serving as a children's pastor. God had miraculously provided.

One Sunday, I was worshipping by the altar in the sanctuary. I noticed a beautiful, petite woman standing at the far end of the altar. I couldn't help but notice her. A few weeks later, I got to meet her face-to-face and discovered that she was more beautiful than I had imagined. "Hi, I'm Louie," I said holding out my hand. I hadn't dated up to that point in time because I was so busy leading the children's ministry, and I knew that I wouldn't date anyone that wasn't a Christian.

She had a great smile and was very poised. "I'm Tricia. I've heard a lot about you and how the church is exploding in growth because of the children's ministry." I laughed, secretly thankful that she knew who I was. She told me how she started visiting the church with her friend. We talked casually over the next few months, but we knew there was chemistry between us.

One day, she shared with me that the Lord had showed her she needed to serve in children's ministry. She was always great with children—they always seemed drawn to her when she was out and about. The moment she stepped into the children's ministry area, the kids were drawn to her there as well. The kids loved her and connected with her. I felt like I had met my best friend, someone who could work alongside me with the kids. Tricia was a brand-new Christian, but her high energy, smiles, and affection made her a magnet for the kids.

During those months that I got to know Tricia and work my dream job, I felt like I was walking in a dream. Then one day, a voice from the past called me with bad news. I had distanced myself from the people and the voices from the South Side. When they called, memories of running the streets of Waukegan and the hopelessness flooded back in.

Chapter 18

GOODBYE POPPI

*The sunset of a person's life speaks volumes as to how
they lived their life. A loved one who lived quietly without
fanfare may seem to have wasted their life. But that life isn't
wasted when they've affected a life that changes another.*

Y ou need to call home," the clerk at Fort Carson Army Base said over
the phone. My dad had been in and out of the hospital during the past
year, and I had taken several trips home. I quickly called my mom and
she said, "Your dad is in the hospital again. They aren't giving him a long
time to live." I didn't know what to do—my heart was in my throat. I went to
the church and a men's meeting was taking place. I pounded on the church
door to talk to Pastor Mark. I knew he could help me. Pastor Mark answered
the church door, and I said, "My dad is dying, and I need to get back home
before he dies."

Pastor Mark pulled together a
group of men, and they prayed for
me. Several put cash in my hand, and
I got in my car. I packed a few things
and drove straight to Waukegan; I
knew I had to get there before it was
too late. When I walked into my
dad's room, he had tubes through his
nose and an IV line linked to his
wrist. He was breathing faintly, and I
grabbed his hand. The hand that
threw a baseball to me and cupped
my hand around a fishing rod, was
now frail in mine.

Dionisio Reyes Sr. was a slim, short man who loved and cared for me
through those difficult years growing up. Wasn't it just yesterday that he
walked into my kindergarten class to take me home? or took me and my
brother fishing at McHenry County Dam? In the last ten years, he was a
mere shadow of who he used to be as the disease from asbestos poisoning

took over his life. He had been homebound, but I still remembered the years we threw a baseball back and forth, and when he taught me how to stand when a baseball was being hurled towards me. Those hot muggy summer nights when he showed me how to hold a baseball bat were gone.

"Dad, this is Louie. I'm here," I whispered in his ear.

Tears came to my eyes, and I began to tell my dad how much I loved him, how much he had taught me, and how much he had done for me. He weakly stroked my head like he use to do when I was a six-year-old boy sitting in his lap. I could see the light fading from his eyes, and I knew that he could go any moment. "Dad, do you know Jesus?" I wanted to make sure I was going to see Dad on the other side of life. He looked up, and he said, "I want to." I led him in a prayer and felt a cloud of peace drift into the room. The weight of life lifted off him, and tears ran down his face. He smiled and then drifted off to sleep. I hugged him and said, "Everything is going to be OK, Pop."

As I sat there seeing my father alive for the last time, I never knew there was more going on behind those eyes I looked into. Although our life was hard, he always seemed to remain steadfast in his love for our mom and us kids. There were secrets that my dad died with that I wouldn't find out until years later. On my mother's death bed twenty years later, she looked at me in tears and said that she had to tell me something. She looked so scared and said to me, "Louie, you will never forgive me for what I am about to tell you."

I looked at her and said, "Mom, I already have forgiven you, and you can tell me anything you need to clear your heart." She looked at me straight in the eye and said, "Your father, Dioniso, who raised you is not your biological father. Your biological father is an African American man, so you are not half Puerto Rican. You are half-black and half-white; we couldn't have children, so your father let me have children with other men so I could have children of my own. I'm so sorry, Louie." Everyone asked me how that made me feel, and this is what I said, "I was overwhelmed with emotion and love for my father, Dionisio. Now I know where I get my love and compassion for children who are not my own;

my father loved me like his own knowing that I was not his biological child, nor were my brother and sister."

My love for my father grew even stronger after that, if only I would have known before my dad died, I would have told him, "Thank you, Pop, for loving me like your own and giving me the same heart to love children that are not my own."

Mom, my brother, and my sister were sitting down around his bed weeping. "Guys, it's going to be OK," I said to them. "Pop is in peace. He isn't in pain. He's going to be OK." My sister started to clear up her tears, and my brother looked up at me. "When you are here, you make everything OK!" He asked me, "What are we going to do?"

I was confused, "What do you mean?" I asked. He looked at Mom, and I realized that they had no idea how they were going to take care of my father's funeral.

I didn't want to talk about this in front of my dad even though he was asleep. "Let's go to Mom's house." We got up and went to their small apartment. My brother and niece were living with my mom and dad. After we sat down, Mom said that Dad had made no arrangements for his funeral. "Louie, we don't know how we're going to pay for it," she said. She glanced meaningfully at Denny.

"I don't have the money, Louie," he said. "I'm working, but I'm trying to get back on my feet." I was the youngest in my family. At twenty-one years old, I was being asked to pay for my father's funeral.

"Of course I'll help," I said trying to ease the strain on my mom and brother. "I'll see what I can do." Suddenly the phone rang. Mom got up and answered it. After she hung up, she turned to us and said that Dad was in a coma. We quickly returned to the hospital. Dad looked peaceful as we walked in. Mom began crying again and holding onto his hand.

I sat down next to him and whispered in his ear: "Dad, you don't have to hold on. You can let go. We'll take care of Mom." His eyes seemed to flutter, or maybe it was exhaustion from no sleep for the past twenty-four hours that was making me see things. I stroked his gray hair like he used to do to me and continued whispering how much I loved him and would miss him, but he needed to let go. "Don't hold on, Pop," I whispered. After quietly weeping, Mom and I decided to go downstairs to get something to drink.

We lived a hard life, and there was a lot of hurt; all we could do now was say, "Goodbye, Pop."

When we walked back onto the elevator to return to my dad's room, the nurse who had been caring for my dad was on the elevator. "I was on my way to get you," she said. "Your dad has died." Mom caught her breath, and I replied, "Thank you. Thank you for taking care of him." The hospital staff was at my dad's bed removing the tubes and IV lines. I looked at Mom, and she looked peaceful. As my family sat around my father weeping, I knew that for some of them looking at his lifeless body, feelings of regret came along with their sadness. We lived a hard life, and there was a lot of hurt; all we could do now was say, "Goodbye, Pop."

My military leadership training kicked into gear, and I knew that I had to take care of the details of the funeral. I had to take command of the situation, like I always had to do with the chaos of my family, and arrange Dad's funeral. I called Pastor Mark from the hospital room. "Pastor Mark, my dad died," I choked up but kept my composure for my family.

Pastor Mark replied, "Brother Louie, this is the time the Holy Spirit does not leave you. The Holy Spirit is right there with you." I felt comfort and strength from those words.

"Thank you, Pastor Mark," I said. "I need to arrange his funeral, and I've never done that before."

Pastor Mark replied, "Don't worry, Louie. I can send you a checklist of what you need to do." He then gave me more advice on what needed to be done in the next twenty-four hours.

I could hardly sleep that night on the couch at Mom's apartment. My brother had gone out with his friends. The next day, Mom woke me up with the smell of frying bacon and eggs. She was still the best cook, and I got up and got dressed. Although we woke up to the reality that Pop has passed the day before, Mom always had that upbeat way about her, even in the midst of crisis. "Eat up, Louie! You're getting too skinny," she said with her boisterous laugh. Then she looked at me and said, "You look good, Louie. It seems like things are going good for you in Colorado. How's your girlfriend, Tricia?"

"She's doing great, Mom," I said. Tricia and I had been dating for a few months; she even got to talk my dad on the phone. "Your dad really liked Tricia," she said. "I do too." I knew my parents would like Tricia, but my mind was on making sure Dad had a proper burial.

We spent the day visiting several funeral homes, filling out forms, and figuring out the program for the funeral. My mom said that Dad had requested that Michael Jackson's song, "Will You Be There?" be played during the funeral. Dad loved to watch *Free Willy* a lot during the last two years and enjoyed the theme song. After talking to the funeral home, I was the only one in the family with a stable income who could secure financing for the funeral, and my budget was $5,000. The only coffin I could afford was called a pauper's box. It was actually a corrugated cardboard box used for the poor. I was heartbroken that I couldn't do more, but since he was a retired veteran, they gave us a folded American flag.

The funeral was at a funeral home in Waukegan. I led the service with a handful of people. For the most part of Dad's life, he was an invalid because of the lung disease that limited his mobility. I was thankful for the few families that joined us, but I was ashamed that Dad was lying in a pauper's box. I asked one of the men who was a military veteran if I could unfold the American flag to drape it over the box to mask that it was a corrugated box. He said I couldn't because a flag was only draped over an active military veteran or someone killed in action. I was still ashamed, and I quietly unfolded the flag and draped it over my dad's cardboard coffin anyway. We buried him without a headstone because we couldn't afford it. As the song, "Will You Be There?" played, I wondered, *Who was this man? What purpose did he have?* I realized that he never got to really live, but he existed and then died. Dionisio Reyes Sr. was a very quiet man who was overcome by a disease because he happened to be working at the wrong place at the wrong time. I realized how brief our lives are on earth, and I wanted to make every second count.

After the funeral, we had a small gathering, and I was eager to get on the road the next day. My brother hugged me and said, "Louie, whenever you come around, you make life better." I was ready to go back to my life with Tricia, Grace Fellowship, and the US Army. Little did I know that in twenty-four months I would return with Pastor Mark to walk the streets of Waukegan.

Chapter 19

HEALING LOVE

*The love of God has the power to erase pain, hurt, and trauma
and liberates us into a life of freedom that may appear impossible.
Marriage is a picture of God's heart for us—a heart of love.*

BURYING MY FATHER and organizing his funeral took a toll on me. I was emotionally exhausted by having to figure out the details of the funeral and navigate the deadly landmines within my family. I returned to Colorado Springs ready for a new chapter. Something inside made me want to build the kind of family that I never had. I wanted to share my life with someone and know that we were going to care for one another through the highs and lows, the good and the bad. I thought of Tricia all the time when I was with my family and wished she was with us. I longed for her presence, and I realized that I wanted her to be a part of my life in every moment.

Tricia knew that I cared for her deeply. I've always been a passionate man; I had shared my heart with her and she understood that I was ready to make a life-long commitment. Initially, Tricia was hesitant about getting into a serious relationship because she was a brand-new Christian. "I'm trying to learn how to be a godly woman," she told me. But I knew that God had brought her into my life. I gave her time and space to pray and seek the Lord about what He would want her to do concerning our relationship, and I settled in my heart to trust Him as well. After about six months, I shared with Tricia about my love for her, and Tricia shared that she was in love with me. God had spoken clearly to us both, and we excitedly began to look forward to our new lives together.

We traveled to Tricia's hometown in New Mexico so I could ask her parents for her hand in marriage. We were both so young. Tricia was twenty-two years old, and I was twenty-three, but her parents gave us their blessing, and we got married in Colorado Springs on July 8, 1995.

We were perfect for one another and did almost everything together. Tricia worked as a retail manager, and I was transitioning out of the military to a full-time children's pastor position. When we weren't working or serving at the church, we enjoyed the outdoors and had a great time exploring all that Colorado Springs had to offer. It was great having someone who not only cared about growing in relationship with me but also growing in relationship with God.

Our marriage wasn't perfect, but it was a healing balm, which God used to minister to the areas of my heart that had been damaged by years of neglect and abandonment. The army had allowed me to feel safe and secure, knowing I had a place to live and a way to take care of myself, but my relationship with Tricia gave my heart rest and peace in knowing that I was accepted and loved in a way that I'd never experienced.

Tricia and I often talked about the future and imagined how God would use our lives for His glory. I told Tricia about the vision that I'd had of a children's ministry that would go into neighborhoods to reach children for Christ. I imagined what it would be like to take the energy, the fun, and the ministry that I was sharing with kids every Sunday, and make it available to children whose parents weren't taking them to church. I pictured myself taking a black metallic truck with a compartment on one side that opened up to a portable stage to do a puppet show in the park for kids. Their smiles, laughs, and joy at hearing the Gospel were just as real to me as if I had experienced it already. I really enjoyed children's ministry, and I wanted to take what I had learned in the church to the parks and streets to reach kids like me who would have followed Jesus if someone had told me about Him. I kept thinking of the hundreds of kids that I grew up with who hung out in the streets of Waukegan and in the broken down parks on the South Side. What if someone brought a quality puppet show, or clown ministry, to young kids? What if that little girl or boy decided to follow Jesus? That little girl and boy could grow up into a leader in their family and community. I could make a difference in the community—I just needed to make a difference in the life of a child.

The answer to so many of the problems in communities starts with the kids, like my friend Gerald who was repeatedly beaten. What if Gerald had met an adult who rescued him from the hands of an abusive stepfather? His life could have been dramatically different because of a caring adult that stepped in when he was a child. I could do it! I could take the Gospel beyond the walls of the church and make an even greater difference for God. There wasn't a whole lot I could do for Gerald, other than be his friend, play Strike Out, and try to comfort him after he'd been hurt by Big John, but in my heart, I knew that I could help other kids.

I had already reached out to Pastor Bill Wilson of Metro Ministries in New York City. I ordered a video tape about his Sidewalk Sunday School Ministry on how to minister to kids in the parks and in rough urban neighborhoods. He was ministering to children in one of the toughest neighborhoods in New York City using a truck with a portable stage on one side with a platform.

When the video tape from Metro Ministries arrived, "That's it!" I shouted to Tricia. "That's what I saw in my vision!" I was overwhelmed that God showed me a picture of a ministry that I didn't even know existed. I realized that I had a plan to carry out what God put in my heart, and God was making things clear to me that I wasn't sure I wanted to see.

As I shared the vision of the truck with Tricia, I never told her about the other burden I was carrying. This vision was foreign and had nothing to do with the children I was reaching in Colorado Springs. I had begun to feel a burden to reach the children of Waukegan, North Chicago, and Zion, Illinois, where I grew up, but I was torn. I didn't want to go back to where I had come from because I loved my life in Colorado Springs. I was married to a gorgeous woman, working in my dream ministry job ,and living in one of the most beautiful cities in the country. Why would I want to leave the mountains of Colorado for the streets of Waukegan to reach kids I didn't know? I thought the idea of reaching kids where I came from must have been a figment of my imagination. Maybe I hadn't really heard from God at all, and I was just being overly zealous. I tried to ignore this pull at my heart, but I could barely sleep at night.

I found the courage to share with Pastor Mark what I was feeling. Being a seasoned pastor, he said, "Let's give it a few months, and if you still feel strongly that you need go back to Waukegan, we will begin the process." After the waiting period, the feelings were even stronger; we needed to go. Pastor Mark shared with the church that God had called me back to my hometown to reach children just like me.

They were sad, yet rejoicing in what God was doing in my and Tricia's life. I knew this was a big step for Tricia, moving further from her family in New Mexico and living in a place where the culture is very different.

Chapter 20

BACK TO WAUKEGAN

Though your beginning was insignificant, yet
your end will increase greatly.

—Job 8:7, nas

O N FEBRUARY 16, 1997, God sent us from Grace Fellowship in Colorado Springs back to Waukegan. The church had blessed us with a $7,000 offering to be used to start our new lives in ministry. Our final service at Grace Fellowship was emotional, with testimonies of how I had made an impact on the lives of the kids. Though I loved the people of Grace Fellowship, I was sure that God had another group of people I was supposed to impact for Him.

I set out to answer God's call to reach kids who were like me on the streets of Waukegan. I felt very blessed as a young man with my smart, beautiful, new wife driving in two cars across the country. I couldn't believe that just five years prior, I had left Waukegan determined to never return. Now I had such a burden to return that it kept me up at night praying and interceding for the kids like Gerald who had no hope and no adult to intervene in their lives. I wondered who Gerald could have become if he had a Christian adult step into his life to rescue him from the hands of his abusive stepfather. If that Christian shared Jesus with Gerald, would Gerald have turned to drugs as an adult, to help him navigate the pain of his past?

Gerald's big eyes haunted me, and I saw the faces of kids that rummaged through garbage cans or the lost and found bins at their schools so they could stay warm with a pair of socks, shoes, or coats in the winter. I was going to reach them, and as we made our way back toward the Midwest, I was confident that God was with me.

The shadow of the Rocky Mountains faded behind Tricia and me as we drove across Nebraska. This was the longest drive that Tricia had ever made in her life, and I kept my eye closely on the rearview mirror watching for her car behind me. We drove long stretches through the Rocky Mountains and then through the plains by night. We stopped along the way to rest, and then continued to press toward the future that waited for us in Illinois.

We'd planned ahead, and had already made arrangements for an apartment in Zion, Illinois, a small town just north of Waukegan. I'd told my family that Tricia and I were moving to the area, and I was surprised at their supportive, excited response. My mom met us at our new apartment at Horizon Village in Zion with a wonderful dinner of roasted turkey, vegetables, and dessert. I think she figured out that we'd had enough fast food on our long trip and wanted a good, home-cooked meal. This was the day that Tricia fell in love with Mom's cooking; she was a great cook! I was so glad to see my mom and was happy to have her as a part of our lives. As we unloaded the boxes out of our two cars, I was thankful that even though the past was challenging, God had given me my mom at this time in my life. It felt good to have a smiling face to welcome me back home.

Things were busy almost immediately as Tricia had set up an interview the next day at a high-end retail store in Lake Forest, Illinois (an affluent suburb of Chicago). Her background in fashion design and merchandising basically guaranteed her the job, and we were hopeful that things would work out. Our plan was for Tricia to work in retail while I established the financial foundation of the church by reaching out and building our adult congregation. I planned to focus on our new church until we were in a position to hire Tricia full-time. For now, we were the first two members of our new church.

While Tricia was at her interview, I had a few hours to pray and ask God what we were supposed to do for our first Sunday in our new city. I sat on the couch with my Bible and thought of the churches we could attend that Sunday. Then as I continued to pray, I stood at the sliding glass door facing the parking lot. A young mom was getting into her car with her younger children. An older man was getting out of his small car that had dents on the door. He bent over, and looked exhausted, likely from working all night.

Suddenly, I heard a voice in my heart. The same presence that I felt when I was that eight-year-old boy in the garage, and when I prayed for Guthrie in the hospital, drifted into the room. I felt a weight behind me and a voice asked, "What did I call you to do?"

I answered, "Start a church."

Then I heard the Lord say, "Well then, start a church." I had no idea how I was going to start a church, but I knew that I at least needed to get the word out!

Suddenly, I could imagine people in our small apartment worshipping God. I saw myself preaching and people responding to an altar call for prayer. I was stirred by God to start the church on Sunday, just a couple of days away. I picked up the phone and called my mom, who seemed to know everybody. "Mom, what are you doing on Sunday?" I knew Mom didn't attend church regularly anywhere. "Nothing. What's going on, Louie?"

I was so excited, "We're having church here, Mom! You gotta come! Invite your friends." By the time Tricia came home from her job interview, I had called everyone I knew to announce our first service on Sunday.

As we stood in the kitchen making dinner to celebrate Tricia's new job, she asked, "Louie, what are we going to do about church on Sunday?"

I hugged her and pulled her close to me, "We're having church here, babe."

She looked up at me surprised. "What?" She asked.

We sat down and I said, "I was praying about what we're supposed to do about Sunday, and God asked me, 'What did I tell you to do?' I immediately knew we're supposed to have our first service on Sunday."

"Where?" she asked.

I threw my arms wide open and laughed, "Here! We're going to have our first service here!"

She looked at the boxes that needed to be unpacked and then asked, "Where are they going to sit? On the floor?" I had not thought that far ahead because I was so excited about hearing God say to start a church in my living room.

"I guess we're going to have to go buy some chairs."

I didn't know how many people were coming, but we decided to buy fifty chairs. Even if just my mom and brother came, I wanted to step out in faith that fifty people could be a part of my brand new church. As we were standing in line at the office supply store, I noticed that the girl standing behind the cashier looked very familiar. "Louie, is that you, Louie?" she smiled. "It's me, Mary Jane from ROTC in high school!"

I almost didn't recognize Mary Jane because she wasn't in her ROTC uniform, and I had not seen her since high school.

"Good to see you, Mary Jane. This is my wife, Tricia." She smiled and waved at Tricia.

"Have you moved back?" she asked. "Yeah, I'm back," I said. She shook her head, "I didn't think you would ever come back when I heard you were living in Colorado Springs. Why did you come back?"

I said, "I'm starting a church."

Mary Jane laughed and said, "Really? I'm looking for a church. Maybe I can check you guys out." I was stunned in that moment by the hand of God in arranging this connection while we were shopping for chairs.

"Are you kidding me?" I laughed, surprised that an old high school friend just happened to be looking for a church. "Then you need to come on Sunday. Here's our address." Tricia handed me a piece of scrap paper and a pen from her purse. "Bring your friends. This is the first service of Church of Joy."

Mary Jane replied, "I will do that. Maybe I can find some of our friends who were in ROTC."

We paid for our fifty folding chairs and then made several trips between the store and our apartment to move them. We stacked the folding chairs in our spare bedroom and prayed over them. We prayed that God would fill those seats with people and that He would draw people on Sunday. We didn't know if three people were coming or thirty, but at least they would have a place to sit if God decided to send them!

Chapter 21

SMALL BEGINNINGS

Whispers from heaven come alive in the hearts of God's people when we respond in faith. Our eyes will show us what's impossible, but our hearts have a capacity for so much more.

O N Sunday, February 23, we set up a hand-made sign created by Tricia on an easel that stated, "Welcome to the Church of Joy." It was our first service, and we lined up thirty of the chairs in several rows, set up an overhead projector to display the lyrics to the songs for praise and worship, and a placed a music stand front and center to hold my notes while I preached. My brother had come with my mom and volunteered to help Tricia lead praise and worship. His job was to press the play button for the Ron Kenoly and Fred Hammond Christian cassette tapes that she would use to lead us in worship. Mom and my high school classmate Mary Jane brought their friends, and we had twenty-two visitors at our first service.

My heart was full of gratitude that God answered so quickly by bringing the people even though I'd only been in town a few days.

After I preached, I led my mom and brother in a prayer of salvation. The hard years of conflict between us that drove me away from Waukegan melted in that moment when God's presence stepped in. I realized that without Him in our midst, we could not be a family. After the service, we enjoyed reconnecting with my friends and family. Hope and faith filled our hearts for the future. If God could bring twenty-two people in three days without any advertising or promotion, what could God do in seven days?

Tricia started her new job as an assistant manager at Talbot's in Lake Forest. I focused on seeking God, meeting people, and getting the word out about Church of Joy. Within a few months, there were too many people in our small apartment every Sunday. The neighbors complained about the noise because most of them were sleeping in when we were worshipping. The landlord had already reminded me several times that I was breaking a rule that limited the number of people I could host for a meeting.

Gang members, drug addicts, and the down and out found hope and life at the Church of Joy.

During those early days of Church of Joy, we witnessed the dramatic transforming power of God. Tricia grew up in a small New Mexico farming town, and our new community was very different for her. She had to adjust to the multi-cultural people that came to our services. One Sunday, a woman in a tight dress came to our church. She kept nodding off to sleep during the service. Because it was obvious that she was having a hard time staying awake, Tricia got her a fresh cup of coffee and asked her how she was doing. "I'm doing fine," she yawned. "I'm sorry, I can barely stay up. It's not because the sermon is boring but because I worked all night." Tricia looked at her, concerned, and asked her if she had not been sleeping well. She yawned again, "No I've been working all night, and I really wanted to be here because my friends told me about the church," she said. Tricia asked, "Where do you work?" She didn't answer but smiled and said she had to go home to rest up because she had to work that night. When Tricia later discovered that she was a prostitute, she was shocked but overcome with compassion for her broken life. Tricia prayed and ministered to this woman several times.

Gang members, drug addicts, and the down and out found hope and life at the Church of Joy. When Jesus set them free from their addictions or a destructive lifestyle, they told their friends who also visited. Soon our small congregation was sitting cramped in our chairs or spilling out into the hallway of our apartment. "Louie, you need to find another place for your church," the apartment manager said as I was paying the rent. "The neighbors are complaining about the noise and how some of your church members are taking their parking spaces. You have to move it, Louie, or I'll have to evict you for breaking the rules. I don't want to evict you because you're a good tenant." I assured her that I was looking for another location, but in my heart, I knew that having too many people was a good problem for a new church to have.

In the meantime, I could hardly sleep because I was thinking of the original reason that God sent me back to Waukegan, which was to reach neglected and hurting kids in their neighborhoods. I spent a lot of time thinking about Bill Wilson's Sidewalk Sunday School in New York City. He was doing my dream—reaching children and changing their lives every day.

I desperately wanted to visit Pastor Bill to learn how he operated his ministry. He was reaching the kids that I wanted to reach and using a method that no one else in the country was doing. His Sidewalk Sunday School was a model for children's outreach around the world and I began praying for a way to make my way to New York City.

In March, I flew out to New York City to see Pastor Bill's ministry, Metro World Child. When I called to make arrangements for my trip, I told his staff that I wanted to see the truck that was in my vision and in *Charisma* magazine. I had been so encouraged by their training video, and I could hardly wait to see their ministry trucks up close. The staff knew I was a new pastor with a minimal budget, so I stayed at the Metro Christian Center in Brooklyn and slept on the floor in one of the rooms of their ministry complex. After a rough night sleeping on the hard floor in an unfamiliar place, I was still excited when I got up the next morning and was invited to attend a staff meeting as if I was part of the team.

Bill Wilson asked me, "Where are you from?"

I said, "I'm from Zion, Illinois."

He said, "I know where Zion is; I've preached there a bunch of times."

I replied, "God has told me to start a ministry to reach children."

He said, "We're going to pray for this young man." He beckoned me to stand up. When I stood up, he prayed, "Lord, I pray that You raise him up to do a great work for children."

> I realized that every children's ministry worker in America owes a debt of gratitude to Pastor Bill, who pioneered making children's ministry the heartbeat of a church and not another program.

The next day we were at another meeting. One of Pastor Bill's assistants came to me and said, "Bill wants to have lunch with you. He must have seen something special in you when he was praying because he never has lunch with anybody. You're somebody special." We walked off, and his assistant took me to an apartment area where Pastor Bill was having Kentucky Fried Chicken for lunch.

As we sat eating fried chicken and coleslaw, Pastor Bill began pouring into me the vision for reaching children. I felt a fire stir within me and wanted to fly back home right then and launch my own Sidewalk Sunday School outreach. I had never met anyone who was so passionate about ministering to children. I realized that every children's ministry worker in America owes a debt of gratitude to Pastor Bill, who pioneered making children's ministry the heartbeat of a church and not another program. Through Pastor Bill, God raised up a model for what He can do when a church's central focus is ministering to children. This was the first church I attended where children's ministry wasn't a secondary program, but a priority. Everything revolved around ministering to every need of the child.

It was Friday and the staff was getting ready to go out to conduct a neighborhood Sidewalk Sunday School. I was assigned to serve on a team, and as we stood outside in our assigned area, a truck came around the corner. "Oh my God," I was overwhelmed with thankfulness. "This was the truck in my dreams." Every emotion erupted within me as I wept. "Are you OK, Louie?" one of the staff asked. "This is the truck that was in my vision," I said. I felt like every hair on my neck was standing up straight as a divine tension collided inside of me—I knew God's will and my will became one in that moment.

I immediately knew how to lead a Sidewalk Sunday School service. Ministering to kids was as natural and easy to me as eating my favorite cereal. I was dumbfounded that God would call me to do something that I loved to do. The rest of the weekend in New York City went by like a blur as I could hardly contain my excitement about getting our first Sidewalk Sunday School truck so we could reach the children in Waukegan.

Chapter 22

BIRTHDAY GIFT

Some of the best gifts in our lives are in the things we give away.
I received something special from those I was called to serve—a
sense of God's calling, presence, and power that was incomparable.

A S EXCITED AS I was about learning from Pastor Bill in New York, I couldn't wait to tell Tricia and our growing church family about all that we were going to do to reach children. I can remember sharing the pictures I had taken in New York and explaining how we could impact children by taking church to the streets instead of waiting on new families to come to us. The members were getting excited and quickly got on board with our first big ministry initiative. Although our church was only two months old, I raised my first special offering to advance God's kingdom. I told the church that we needed $5,000 to launch our Sidewalk Sunday School outreach, and we only raised $3,000. I wasn't disappointed because I thought we were doing pretty well for a new congregation comprised of working-class people. We had no millionaire types sitting in our church waiting to write us a big fat check. We had to believe and work with what God had given us.

I was determined that if I had to donate blood to get the money, we were going to get a truck to reach the kids in Waukegan. The first Sidewalk Sunday School truck cost $2,000, and we spent the rest of the special offering money on sound equipment and supplies. God had given me an unmistakable faith that if I worked hard to do His will, His power would join our efforts.

While we were getting the truck ready, we were also moving into our new location at Beulah Park Elementary School. The landlord at my apartment building said our church needed to be out of our apartment as soon as I came back from New York, and I was thankful that we had a temporary location in the elementary school until we could figure out a permanent place for our new church. Once we finalized our move into Beulah Park Elementary School, we focused on preparing the truck for our first Sidewalk Sunday School service.

By June, we had purchased a box truck that had been used for deliveries for the Joseph Floral Company; Denny, other men from the church, and I worked to modify the truck with new paint and carpeting. We didn't have anywhere to park it, so we parked it outside of our apartment. The last touch that the truck needed was an eye-catching, attractive design. Tricia and I were out of money, and we couldn't afford to hire a designer or to buy the artwork for the truck. "So how do you think we should design the truck?" Tricia asked me.

"I'm trying to remember how we handled creating giant drawings for the children's ministry stage at Grace Fellowship," I told Tricia. Suddenly I had a vision of myself back at Grace Fellowship on a Saturday afternoon. I had an overhead projector and a transparency with a drawing. I was projecting the drawing onto a wall with a giant piece of cardboard attached to the wall. I saw myself drawing a giant David and Goliath on the cardboard. I realized that I could take that same principle to create an illustration on the side of the truck.

"I got it Tricia," I said. "Remember how we used to draw those giant cutout characters on the wall at Grace Fellowship?

She nodded, her eyes brightening. "Yeah I remember! We would project the drawing onto the wall and then color the giant characters on the cardboard." We had a plan and Tricia created the artwork on a transparency. The next night we were in the parking lot with black Sharpie markers tracing the outline of "Sidewalk Sunday School" and three smiling clowns on the side of our truck. Several of our church members came over the next day and filled in the design with exterior paint.

I was full of adrenaline and could hardly sleep those nights as I dreamed of how God was going to use Sidewalk Sunday School to reach kids like Gerald and me. One night, God spoke to me to pray and drive through the areas where we wanted to reach out. We drove through some of the roughest areas of Waukegan and North Chicago, spraying the streets with anointing oil. We prayed that we could take the streets for Christ. We knew there wasn't any power in the oil, but we were doing a symbolic act to stir our faith. We declared our hope that Sidewalk Sunday School would change the lives and destinies of children who had no hope and no future.

While Tricia worked, I spent days walking through neighborhoods and knocking on every door in the projects. I knew that if a mom didn't meet me personally, she would not trust me to minister to her child. These families couldn't just be handed a flyer. Parents had to know the people behind the flyer so that they wouldn't just send their kids one time. I wanted something long term. I wanted to build relationships with the people in the community because in a rough neighborhood, it takes a lot to prove to people that you want to give them something wonderful without expecting anything in return. On Saturdays, a couple of neighborhood kids would meet me and help me go door to door passing out flyers and getting the word out about Sidewalk Sunday School. I think I knocked on the door of every housing project in Waukegan and North Chicago.

"Hey, Pastor Louie," one mom called out my name as I passed her apartment, "Lakiesha can't wait for Sidewalk Sunday School. When are you going to have it?" she asked while blowing smoke from her cigarette.

"Next Saturday," I said. "We're having it at King Park. Hope to see you there!"

She waved and said, "I'll send Lakiesha and her friends, Pastor Louie. I'm too far gone for God."

I replied, "You're never too far gone."

She shut the door.

I told every kid in the projects that I would blow a siren as a signal that Sidewalk Sunday School was starting. When I drove down the first street, crowds of kids came running towards the truck. I stopped the truck, rolled the window down and yelled, "Hey, I need to drive around and let the rest of the kids know that Sidewalk Sunday School is starting at King Park. Wait for me at the park!" I waved the kids away and continued driving down the streets in the projects.

When we pulled the truck up to King Park to the throngs of kids, I could not believe the turnout and that I was about to do what had been in my heart for several years. I had to hold back tears when I looked at the faces of thirty boys and girls who were just like me, wandering the streets and alleys of Waukegan trying to avoid the poverty and the violence. Which boy is like Gerald, trying to survive a violent family member? Which girl is like my sister's friend Angie, who was shot one night? My heart beat fast because I knew that the next hour could change their future forever.

Kids started climbing into the truck. "What are you doing?" I asked one little boy.

"We're getting in to watch the show," he said.

"No, you need to sit on the grass," I said. "The show isn't in the truck. I'm going to do the show in the park."

He laughed and smiled, and told the rest of his friends to go sit on the grass. Laughter, giggles, and joy erupted as I stepped out of the truck. We let down the portable stage as music blared in the background like a call beckoning the curious. Children came from everywhere, and we started our service. We played games, and I taught a lesson and told a Bible story. It was July 12, my twenty-sixth birthday, and the kid's didn't know God had given me a party where they were the honored guests. The moments when God touched the hearts of those girls and boys were God's birthday present to me. This was the best birthday party I had ever had in my life. Little did I know, some of my future ministry leaders were sitting cross-legged in that crowd.

Chapter 23

DON'T QUIT

He took a little child and had him stand among them. Taking
him in his arms, he said to them, "Whoever welcomes one of
these little children in my name welcomes me, and whoever
welcomes me does not welcome me but the one who sent me."
—MARK 9:36–37, NET

T HE CHURCH QUICKLY outgrew Beulah Park Elementary School and
we soon needed a bigger facility. I found an abandoned warehouse on
the corner of Elisha Street and 27th Avenue in Zion. The rent was four
times what we were paying at Beulah Park Elementary School, but I knew
God was more than able to help us pay the $4,000 per month. The building
had 30,000 square feet and needed a lot of work, but when I walked into
the expansive building, I envisioned offices, a game room, and a sanctuary
featuring a Nickelodeon-style game show set with colorful characters and
giant TV monitors hanging up throughout the room to broadcast the service.
I wanted to bring the excitement and wonder of God to kids who would
tune out a traditional sermon if it wasn't accompanied with the high-quality
production excellence they were accustomed to seeing on TV. When you put
excellence into presenting the gospel, you're sending a message to that child
or teenager that they are so valuable to God, that He wants to reach them.

In the midst of making great advancements with the ministry, Tricia and I
also bought our first home through the VA loan program for military families.

Not only was our ministry growing, our family was too! We were expecting our first child, and Tricia spent her days either helping out with our thriving church or setting up our new home. Although she was offered a management position at her retail job, we were so busy ministering to families that she turned down the promotion to join the ministry administrative team.

Things were moving along well. Members of the church were working hard to help me scrub, clean, empty, and paint our new church building. I was busy at the church and helping Tricia at home. As we planned to open our doors in July, Tricia went into labor the week before. I found myself running back and forth from the church to the hospital. We were seeing new life spring forth in the hearts of our members as God used us to prepare His house and share something special with our community. It was great to see how God had done so much, so quickly, and we were all excited about what was ahead. Tricia and I welcomed our daughter, Madison, into our hearts and into our family. I had everything I'd ever wanted and our lives were overflowing with gratitude.

Church of Joy became the happening church at that time and we experienced significant growth within our adult congregation. However, it seemed like every time we were increasing, something would get thrown at us to try and set us back.

warfare

So much was happening in the church and in our family, that the growth of the Sidewalk Children's Ministry was inevitable. Our consistent presence in the roughest neighborhoods had caused us to gain the respect of many families, whether they had children who were young enough to attend our programs or not. Sidewalk Sunday School became a normal part of neighborhood life and the sound of our siren was as easily recognized as any commercial jingle on television. The children heard our sirens and came running to the park every week without fail.

As the ministry was going well with a growing congregation and a thriving ministry outreach to the children, God showed me that I had a split vision. I knew God had called me to reach children, but I didn't know who was going to pay for it or support it. I either had to commit my resources, talents, and focus to reaching children or to the adult congregation.

After we settled into our new church building, we began to hear something new from the children that we hadn't heard before. One Saturday in King Park, the kids gathered around me and began to ask, "Pastor Louie, when can we come to church?"

I was puzzled at first, and said, "What do you mean? We just had Sidewalk Sunday School—we had church!"

"No!" the kids began, "We want to come to your church—to your building."

I didn't know what to do. I wasn't sure in that moment how to respond, but I knew that I'd have to come back the following week with a real answer. What was I going to do with the hundreds of children that were worshipping with us in the park? How was I going to get them, with or without their parents, to our church services?

As I walked the usual neighborhoods that week, passing out flyers and doing visitation, I asked around and found that children wanted to attend the outdoor Sidewalk Sunday School services *and* come to church. So, my solution was to start bussing the children to our church on Sunday morning. It seemed like an exciting mission, and God's people love to reach out. I began to share the vision with our adult congregation and the impact we could continue to make bussing these children. The congregation loved it at first. I raised money in our adult congregation to purchase three buses; it was a miracle. Our church rallied around this effort and gave $24,000. We purchased the three buses and decided to bus the children to our church on Easter Sunday. I never would have imagined that so many young people would be willing to stand outside their homes, waiting on the church bus to pick them up on Sunday morning.

As the year went on, the outreach continued to grow in spite of the winter weather. Normally, Sidewalk Sunday School would only happen when the weather was warm enough for us to share the ministry outside in the parks, but since we were now holding services in our new building, there was no break in our outreach. In the middle of winter, there were children as young as three and four years old waiting in sub-zero weather for the bus to pick them up to take them to church. The kids knew that if they could make it to Sidewalk Sunday School, they would be warm, have fun, and at least have a chance to get something to eat from people who cared about them. It was rough for children from the projects; a lot of their parents were either drunk or strung out on drugs with no interest at all in going to church.

As we continued to bus the children to our church, we saw how much more we were impacting them. We had teenagers as well wanting to come to church. We launched our midweek service to the children and teenagers. It started out small; however, over time it began to grow significantly.

When we picked up kids on the buses, we usually didn't have any problems. There were moments when a fight broke out between groups of kids because they were from rival cities (which we quickly learned to identify). We called the police a few times to the bus when the fights broke out into a mob brawl. I was very strict about safety standards, and if we knew who the perpetrator was of the fight, they were banned from the bus. We asked our adult congregation to help monitor the kids when they arrived, got off the buses, and filed into the sanctuary.

After our midweek service for the children and teenagers, I noticed a group of boys gathering in the game room. Suddenly, I heard yelling, and they were pushing one another. Six to eight boys that were the same size as me were punching and kicking each other. I was so concerned about the safety of the smaller kids who looked frightened watching this fight that I grabbed a couple of the kids and carried them outside. My security guard, Angel Guzman, tried to break up the fight while I grabbed kids and carried them outside.

When I put one boy down, his father pulled up in an older Chevrolet, and he screamed at me, asking what was I doing with his son. I didn't stay to respond but went back inside to pick up and carry more kids out. As I stepped out the door, I noticed that he was carrying a gun. I stopped and said, "Hey man, I was trying to make sure your son is safe. We're trying to break up a fight inside." His son looked up at him and said, "Dad, that's Pastor Louie, and he was trying to help me." Police sirens were screeching and the young father put his gun back in his pocket and told his son to get in the car.

The police finally showed up to break up the fight. That fight was one of many spontaneous riots that erupted before or after a service. I was becoming frustrated and felt like I was working harder to save these kids from the streets than their parents, educators, or any other adult in their lives. The tension between the adult congregation and managing the hundreds of children and a handful of teenagers with ties to the gang lifestyle began to take its toll on the church.

I was a new dad, pastor, and children's pastor, and my focus was on the children. Tricia and I had spent hours training the adult congregation to lead. After several leadership-training sessions, we thought that we had a solid leadership team who understood our heart and what it would take to reach and make a difference in the communities we were trying to impact.

One Saturday while I was setting up for Sidewalk Sunday School at King Park, I wondered why I hadn't seen some of my adult team members who normally volunteered to help. I asked Juanita, a staff member, to call them while I was setting up the stage. "Pastor, all I'm getting are voicemails," she said. "I've left messages, but I don't think they are coming." Juanita and I pushed through holding the service without our volunteers while hiding the sadness and frustration we felt about our adult members who told me that they wanted to help out, but had gone missing in action. Leaving voicemails and unanswered calls became the norm. I realized that the adults were ignoring my calls even though they said they wanted to reach children.

"I'm not coming back to your church," said one member after a Sunday service. He was one of the men who had been a big help in our church as our congregation continued to grow. I couldn't believe what I was hearing because I thought he would have been one of my key leaders in our rapidly exploding children's ministry. He was one of the adults that I called on a few Saturdays wondering why he wasn't keeping his commitment to reaching kids in the park.

"Why?" I asked him.

"I don't want my kids around those kids that we pick up from the projects," he said. "They cuss and act up, and I don't want my kids to be around them. Furthermore, I refuse to use my Cadillac Escalade as a taxicab for these kids," he continued, throwing in a few choice words.

I couldn't believe how these members, that once said they would stand by our side, forever reaching these children, were cussing the ministry out, leaving, and on top of that, asking for their tithes and offerings back. One particular member said, "I want all of my tithes and offerings back because I didn't sign on to this. I thought I was coming to a church, not a place where I had to get a commercial driver's license and show up every Saturday to help out with Sidewalk Sunday School."

This member was upset as I explained to him that his tithes and offerings went into the General Fund, and we could not return his money. He suddenly stood up and cussed me out, shouting profanities that everyone in the church foyer could hear. With the slam of the door, he left my life forever.

People who said they wanted to be members suddenly closed their bank accounts, so tithe checks wouldn't clear. One member wrote a check for $500, which didn't clear. We usually redeposited the check a week after it bounced, but it still didn't clear. Tricia called the person, and they said they had deliberately shut down their checking account because they didn't want the check to clear. "I'm going to sue you for all of the tithe checks that I wrote out to your ministry," the woman threatened Tricia.

We were feeding the children every Sunday; we would send them a snack bag filled with a sandwich and juice drink. Members would help purchase the food and make the sandwiches the night before for the children. One Sunday morning, a woman came in with some of the sandwiches, the rest were not done. She threw the loaf of bread, turkey, and cheese on the counter and said angrily, "Here, Pastor Louie, here are your sandwiches; I didn't have time to make them!" It was sad to see the people hard and resentful toward the children. What happened to Christianity?

I was hurt and stunned—when hundreds of kids were accepting Christ as their Savior and wanting to learn more about God, our adult congregation was dwindling and falling apart. The hostility of former members, who stopped attending and giving, robbed funding for the fuel and buses that kids needed to get to church. Soon, the Sunday morning service was overrun by children, and I was doing most of the work with a small group of adult volunteers. Every week, I would conduct a small service with the remaining adults and families; many times Tricia and I would have to pick the children up, and when I got back, I jumped into the pulpit to preach. As soon as service was over, I would drive the children home on the bus. I was completely overwhelmed, and I was amazed at how quickly our ministry unraveled.

I prayed and asked God for direction and realized that I needed to know who was with me and who wasn't with me. I knew that I made it clear in the messages from the first service that my vision was to reach the children of the projects of Waukegan and North Chicago. I didn't want to build another typical church. I wanted to create a church that I would attend if an adult asked me to when I was playing baseball or running the streets at ten or eleven years old. There was no way I would abandon a generation who had responded so powerfully to God.

I knew I had to do something drastic. I couldn't afford to wonder week to week about where I stood with those who called me their pastor. I canceled a Sunday service and sent a letter and a cassette tape, which shared the vision God gave me to reach children, to every member asking them not to attend the following Sunday service if they were not with us, committed to reaching the kids. At that time, we needed every adult in the congregation to accept a volunteer job of either monitoring the kids when they arrived or departed from the church, driving the bus, or helping out with Sidewalk Sunday School services. It was clear to everyone that my heartbeat was in reaching the children, so I assumed that if they became members, they had the same vision for reaching children.

By the following Sunday, our adult congregation had dwindled from two hundred adults to a handful. I was devastated, but I didn't let the kids see my heartbreak at our Sunday morning service. The remaining adult members led an upbeat service sharing the good things God wanted to do in the kids' lives and encouraging them not to take drugs and to stay off the streets. The kids loved the message and never wanted to leave the service. It's a day I'll never forget. I smiled on the outside, but I broke when I dropped off the last child at their home that afternoon.

With most of our adult congregation gone, the funding dropped dramatically, and Tricia and I had no other choice than to quit paying ourselves in order to fund our ministry to children.

In crisis, I called the only person I knew who could identify with what we were trying to do. Hoping for an answer, I called Pastor Bill at Metro Ministries in New York City. When I called, I was shocked that he answered the phone. His staff usually answered his phone and transferred me if he was available. I considered the fact that he answered the phone a miracle. I spilled everything to Bill, going on and on about how we were ready to lose everything. I somehow thought that he'd have an answer, a way out, some way to help us; instead he yelled, "Don't quit!" and hung up.

I put my face in my hands, and Pastor Bill's words rang in my ears. After all I'd shared, the last thing I expected to hear was "don't quit." Those words, however, would come back to me often over the following weeks of trying to reach God's children, pulling them from the streets, luring them from the gangs, and offering them a future we knew we couldn't afford. Because we were causing young people to choose life and reject the gangs, drugs, and violence that had been a part of their lives, I had death threats from parents and drug dealers.

Local pastors invited me to a lunch, only to wrap up the meal by circling around me, telling me what a mistake I'd made by bringing street kids into the church. A much-known pastor, locally, told me that I shouldn't be living this way and out of God's will. One prominent pastor from out of town, who I had once admired, said, "Your ministry is a dying cow, shoot it in its head and let it out of its misery." We'd have people calling our church offices, telling us to quit because we were not in God's will. Rumors spread about our leadership style and our requirement of having our members help serve the children. I didn't think it could get any worse, and then it did.

We called our pastor, Mark Cowart, and with tears I asked him, "Pastor, tell me what to do"? Pastor Mark stayed quiet for a moment, then replied, "Brother Louie, all I can tell you is that sometimes a seed has to go into the ground before it is resurrected." I thank God for Pastor Mark; he didn't tell me I was out of God's will or to quit. He and his wife Linda encouraged us, prayed for us, and were there if we needed them.

Chapter 24

LOSING EVERYTHING

Those who try to gain their own life will lose it; but
those who lose their life for my sake will gain it.
— MATTHEW 10:39, GNT

S OMEONE WAS BANGING on my door and men were shining flashlights
outside our bedroom windows. The piercing light breaking through
the darkness in my bedroom and pounding fists banging on the walls
awakened Tricia and me out of sleep. I thought someone was trying to break
into our house. I put my robe on and went to the door. I opened the door
and a large man in jeans and a T-shirt with tattooed arms pushed a piece
of paper in my face. "We're here to get your truck," he yelled. I said, "Listen,
you don't have to get rude with me. Let me get the keys and clean out my
truck before you take it." I looked at the men that were holding flashlights
outside of my window and said, "And tell them to stop that. You're scaring
my wife and daughter."

He stepped back and yelled, "Just give us the truck!" I closed the door, and
he yelled again, "Don't lock the door on us. We're not going away. We'll stay
here until you have to leave tomorrow morning." I yelled back at him, "I'm
not going to lock my door. I'm going to get my keys so I can clean out the
truck!"

I was furious that I was in this situation—with these repossession goons
showing up at my house at 1:00 a.m. to take my truck. "Where are you God?"

I said under my breath. I pulled my jeans and T-shirt on and grabbed my keys. "Stay inside," I told Tricia as I walked out. I got into my truck and cleaned out the glove compartment and grabbed Madison's toys and hair clips out of the back of the seat. I was humiliated that the bank repossessed my truck. I called Cheryl, a member of our staff, for an emergency meeting at the church. "My truck got repossessed," I told Cheryl, Tricia, and another staff person as we stood in the sanctuary. I didn't want to hold anything back because they knew the stark truth of our situation. We were shaken by the middle-of-the-night visitor, but we were determined to continue with the ministry.

We still had Tricia's truck, and one day while driving home, something rose up in me: I wanted to drive it off the road. "I just want to flip this truck," I told Tricia angrily. A darkness had taken over me, and I didn't want to live. With the chaos of kids who brought in their gang influence, a dwindling congregation of adults, no money, and pastors in the community telling me that this was not God's will, I felt abandoned and forsaken by God. Death looked more attractive. When I got home, I went and closed myself in the bedroom to I read my life insurance policy. I had resigned that I was ready to die, but I wanted to make sure Tricia and Madison would be taken care of. When I read the policy, I realized that I was worth more dead than alive.

After Tricia put Madison in bed, I told her matter-of-factly that I planned on killing myself. "You and Madison will be taken care of," I said. "I'm worth more dead than alive, and I might as well die."

Tricia sat next to me and tears came to her eyes, "You don't really mean that, Louie."

I turned over and said, "Tricia, God has forsaken me. He's left me. Maybe all those people who are saying that this isn't God are right. Maybe I totally missed it."

I was mad at God that the kids I was praying and fighting for were fighting among themselves. I thought I had done everything God wanted me to do, and everything was blowing up around me. I was getting death threats from angry parents and lawsuits filed against me by bill collectors. We had received several notices that our home was facing foreclosure. Sleep took over as I fought emotional exhaustion.

I quit wanting to preach or go to the services. I went through the motions to reach the kids during Sidewalk Sunday School services, but inside I felt the same sense of abandonment that haunted me when my family left me at sixteen years old. I was reliving the horrible feeling of walking into my apartment after getting out of the hospital and finding nothing but trash strewn across the floor, my clothes, and a handwritten note: "Louie, go live with your friends." Was God writing me a note, sending a message that He had left with the death threats, creditor notices, piles of bills, and local pastors telling me to leave because I was out of His will?

I hid this war from the hundreds of children that continued to come to the Sidewalk Sunday School services and the handful of adults that supported the vision. But Tricia was too close to my war zone. She was so close that when she came home from the church each day, she would leave Madison in the truck and come inside to make sure I had not killed myself. I kept a revolver in the house and pulled it out several times. Shooting myself would take just seconds, and the pain from betrayal, shame, and abandonment would be over.

Tricia found me sleeping most of the time. I was exhausted from dealing with the constant harassment of creditors and the heavy workload left by former members who spread rumors and accusations about my character. When Tricia and I had dinner after working at the office, I would turn to her and tell her, "Tricia, let's go. Let's shut this down. God isn't in this; it's so obvious. We can move to New Mexico where you can be close to your parents."

Every time, Tricia answered, "No, I'm not leaving. I'm not walking with you in your disobedience." I was so mad at her that I would get up and walk out. I was trapped in this war zone and death seemed to be the only way out. Soon, her truck was also repossessed, and I thought she would relent to moving to New Mexico, but she didn't. Instead, she arranged for us to borrow a church van until we could buy a vehicle. At that point, the ministry was so poor, I had to siphon diesel fuel from a broken down bus into a can to fuel another bus; I didn't see any opportunity of buying a vehicle in the future. I was familiar with the biting taste of diesel fuel that hit my mouth when I blew through the hose into the gas tank in order to get the fuel from bus to bus on that dreary fall day. We couldn't even afford to pay a mechanic to fix the bus, so a teenager who had experience hot-wiring cars when he was running the streets helped me figure out how to fix it.

My church mechanic was a former car thief. We had no cars, and we couldn't afford to buy groceries. We were losing everything and eating from the food pantry in the church. We were hungry and nearly homeless, just like I was when I lived in Waukegan many years before. I hated that life, and now I was tasting the desperation of lack again. I didn't see any answers or way out of this endless tunnel. One late morning, after Tricia and Madison had left the house, I pulled out the revolver and fingered the barrel and put it in my mouth. Just one push of the trigger, and I could finish this nightmare.

Chapter 25

THE NIGHTMARE ENDS

*We often don't realize how much we hold the reigns
to controlling the madness in our lives. God is always
there. Faithful. Never changing. Ever strong.*

A S I TASTED the cold steel barrel of the revolver in my mouth, in my mind, I suddenly saw Madison as a teenager. She was crying and hopeless, depressed, and sad because she had no father. Then I saw Tricia without me, struggling and in despair. The pictures of Madison's crying and Tricia's despair moved me to tears. I cried with the revolver's barrel in my mouth, and I pulled it out. I fell to the floor sobbing and pounded the floor. "God where are you?" I screamed at the ceiling. "Where are you? Why have you forsaken me?" I didn't get any answers, but the overwhelming sadness of losing Madison and Tricia and the bleak future my suicide would create made me wipe the tears off my face and get up.

I'd gathered my emotions by the time Tricia returned home, but I knew in my heart that I had to find a way out of the darkness and depression. A couple of days later, Tricia announced that she had something that would help me. Tricia surprised me and said that she had scheduled an appointment for us to visit a counselor. Once she finally coerced me into getting into the church van, I kept reminding her of how I was a failure and that a counselor couldn't help. I didn't want to see a counselor, and she kept getting lost in the busy Chicago streets as she tried to find the counselor's office. I grumpily told her to forget trying to find the counselor and was overwhelmed with sleep. I fell asleep and when I woke up about thirty minutes later, she was parked in front of the counselor's office. Although my attitude hadn't changed, I thought I would go through the motions of the visit for Tricia's sake. I had no intention of getting any help from him. I was convinced that he had no idea what I was going through.

When we walked into the counselor's office, his friendly assistant escorted us into a beautifully decorated, comfortable consultation room with several leather couches and a glass table in the middle with a stack of books. The counselor introduced himself to us, and I acknowledged him; I then settled myself on the couch in silence. Tricia explained to him what was happening and the symptoms that I was battling. The counselor then explained that my symptoms were classic signs of depression. "When you lose serotonin, you're in a down state," he explained. "That's why you're battling the constant fatigue and tiredness. You're mentally and physically in a down state."

I leaned forward and asked, "Well, how do I get out of this?" He suggested medication, and I laughed, telling him, "I'm not big on medications, doc."

He smiled and replied, "Well, the only way you can get out of this is by choosing to come out of this."

I was surprised by his answer and asked, "Are you saying that I can end this today if I choose to?"

He nodded and said emphatically, "Absolutely, Louie. You can end the depression today if you choose to come out of it."

I realized that I had the power to change my perspective from the Bible verse, Philippians 4:13—that I can do anything through Christ who strengthens me. I chose His strength in my weakness in that moment. I asked the counselor about my struggle to continue preaching when I didn't feel like it. He said, "If you don't want to preach Louie, then don't preach. Aren't there other members of your staff who can step in to preach when you don't want to?" I instantly thought of Cheryl, who was highly regarded by the congregation. She was in tune with God, intelligent, and a gifted speaker. Cheryl or Tricia would be perfect for stepping in when I didn't want to preach.

Suddenly the weight of carrying the battle for the ministry lifted, and I felt free. I felt free to think clearly about our options, and I had hope that we had a future. The darkness that I had walked in was gone when I walked out of his office. The sun looked brighter, and I felt hope that we could get through this. I didn't know how we were going to pay the creditors, but I was determined that every one of them would be paid in full, even if it took the rest of my life to pay them back.

I felt hope again, even when we had one of our children's services interrupted by a police officer serving a subpoena for a lawsuit. The company that filed the lawsuit against us was a Christian-owned business. The next day Tricia and Cheryl called every creditor and explained our situation. The responses we received were the opposite of what I expected. The rest of the businesses that were not Christian-owned were willing to work with us.

When Tricia showed me the letter from the bank notifying us of the foreclosure on our home, I had a plan in the back of my mind on how we could slowly recover from our financial crisis. "Honey, I got the final notice that the bank is foreclosing on our house," Tricia told me over breakfast. "What are we going to do?" I had an idea, but I was still looking for a place that we could either afford or that had a landlord who offered flexible payment terms. "I've got a few properties that we can drive over to look at," I said optimistically. Our adult congregation had dwindled down to a handful; we were completely broke. At this time, Tricia and I were still not receiving paychecks.

"One option is to move into the basement," I suggested. She shook her head and laughed. "It's dark and creepy down there," she said. "There's no way I would live there."

Madison was pulling at my shirt and wanted me to pick her up. I loved being a dad to my beautiful little girl. I had to hold back tears thinking of what would happen if we didn't get out of this hole. I didn't want Madison to taste the poverty I had endured as a child. I wanted her to have a completely different life than I had growing up.

Her big eyes looked up at me as she held out her arms, waiting for me to scoop her up in a big hug like I always did every morning. I picked her up and tickled her. She laughed and for a moment, I forgot about the hard decision ahead of me with figuring out where we were going to live.

Tricia and I looked at some properties, but she soon realized that we could not even afford to pay rent. While driving away from another property that we couldn't afford, I looked her in the eye and said, "Tricia, it's just what we have to do. But I promise I'll make it as homey as possible for you and Madison." I said this matter-of-factly, but inside I was crumbling. I hated the fact that my wife and daughter would live in the basement of the church that was in a sketchy area. Tricia looked out the van window while Madison was sleeping in her car seat. "We will live there, just for a season, until the ministry gets back on its feet," I said quietly.

The next day, I walked downstairs to the basement of the church. Metal pipes and wires hung from the exposed ceiling and the cement walls were splattered with oil and chemicals of different colors. I closed my eyes, and I saw colorfully painted walls, carpet under my feet, a living room, and kitchen area. With a drop ceiling, sheet rock, carpet, and quality lighting, this smelly cold basement could be a home.

I called a few guys from the church who had helped out with construction projects in the past. None of them wanted to help. We were getting close to having to move out of our home and I prayed that God would send me the right people for this project or tell me whom to call. One day Tricia told Madison's babysitter, Kathy about our struggle to find someone to help with the renovation project. Kathy turned to Tricia and said, "My husband is a carpenter. I'll ask him if he can help." Tricia told me about Kathy's husband, and I knew he might be our last hope because no one else was willing.

I put together a list of tasks and started cleaning the basement. While sweeping the piles of dirt into a heap, a heavy-set Caucasian man with a cigarette hanging out of his mouth walked down the basement steps, right into my path. I looked up at him and wondered if he was another bill collector. "I'm sorry man, but I can't pay you right now," I said standing up straight. "You're going to get paid, but I need a little more time." He laughed and said, "I'm not here to get a bill paid. My wife, Kathy, said you might need some help with carpentry."

I wiped the sweat from my brow and breathed in deeply. Finally, God answered my prayer. I reached out my hand, "I'm Pastor Louie," I said. He smiled and said, "I don't have to be a member of your church to help you right?" I shook my head, "No, you don't have to be a member." He looked at the walls, "Good, because me and God have a lot to work out. But I wanted to help you, and you look like you can use it." Carl came by every day, after putting in a full day of work at his regular job, to help me put up sheet rock and finish the walls of our new home.

Carl was a smoker and cussed every time he accidentally hit his fingers with a hammer. I didn't care at this point and welcomed any help. If God could make a donkey talk in the Bible, He could send anyone into my life to further His cause. After years of dealing with Christians who said they wanted to help but abandoned me, and non-Christians who were willing to put in hours after working a full-time job, I was going to embrace whomever God sent into my life.

Soon Carl brought some of his friends to help wire the lighting, lay carpet, and install plumbing for the kitchen area. Tricia sketched out a floor plan and showed me color swatches for the different rooms. I showed her plans to Carl. "This looks really nice, Pastor Louie," he said while smoking his cigarette.

"Yeah, Tricia really knows how to create a color scheme and make any place look like home," I laughed. I didn't tell Carl, but I had no money to finish what she had sketched out.

The next day, Carl and his friends showed up with the materials. "How much do I owe you, Carl?" I asked. He waved his hand and said, "Don't worry about it. I got it." The materials that Carl bought were perfect finishing touches on the space. Madison's bedroom was painted purple just like she asked, and Tricia had the lighting that she wanted in our bedroom. The dark, smelly basement was transformed into a small apartment area with a living room, kitchen, bathroom, and two bedrooms. Our basement apartment wasn't fancy, but it was home and would help with building our financial future by eliminating an impossible mortgage payment.

As soon as we moved in, Tricia and I decided that I needed to go on the road to share the vision of reaching children with other churches in the nation. I bought a video-editing machine with some money from small donations that were still coming in from friends at Grace Fellowship in Colorado. In one evening, I taught myself how to use the machine, and I stayed up late every night for two weeks putting together the first Sidewalk Sunday School video. After I completed the video, I prayed and sent a copy to a pastor I knew in North Carolina and asked him if I could come speak at his church. The pastor was so moved by the video, he called and invited me to speak to his church.

On the day of my trip, our church had ninety dollars in the bank, and since I'd be gone on a Sunday, we would still have church for the kids. I had already discontinued adult services several months prior, so we only held one service on Sundays. When the adults left the church, and I emerged from my depression, God had shown me that I still had a staff of volunteers who would make the outreach to children and teens a reality. For a few months, I selected and trained young people to form a Teen Leadership group that helped with everything in the church from answering phones and cleaning and setting up for services to monitoring buses and teaching in classrooms.)

Before I left for the airport, I gathered our teen leaders and said, "Dad is leaving and Mom is here. Your job is to take care of Mom." These were our kids from the streets, and they all understood that we were family. I exhorted them to help Tricia and the other adults monitor the services and do whatever was needed to serve the kids. Their eyes were wide open, but I knew they were ready for this moment. I had spent hours conducting training sessions using excellent leadership curriculum. They had no idea who John Maxwell was, but I poured into them his principles of leadership and serving. They received the same training as any C-level executive at a secular company. Although some of them were only twelve years old, I knew they were ready to take on more responsibility for the health of our church. With that encouragement, Tricia and Madison would drive me to the airport every weekend to see if there were others out there who wanted to make a difference in children's lives.

Chapter 26

SPEAK FOR THE VOICELESS

I didn't know that God had prepared me to speak for those who could not speak for themselves. My own story of poverty gave me a voice that could not be easily silenced.

P ASTOR BILL HAD been reaching over 100,000 children every week in New York City. God was using Him in an awesome way, and we were so encouraged when he invited Tricia and me to a weeklong staff retreat. Every year, Bill gathered his staff to cast vision and share the latest children's ministry techniques as well as provide a time to connect with like-minded leaders. I was eating lunch along with him and his staff and said, "Bill, I'm starting to travel and share the vision of how we're reaching children in the Chicagoland area."

He put a piece of his chicken down on the plate and motioned for me to sit next to him. "You need to travel with me," he said. I was honored by the invitation but didn't have the extra money to travel with him in addition to the trips I had already booked. "I don't know, Bill. I need to think about this because money is tight."

He said, "You just buy your plane ticket, and I'll take care of your hotel, car, and food." Pastor Bill's invitation turned into a three-year season of meeting him in cities around the country and accompanying him when he ministered or went to leadership meetings.

I would meet Pastor Bill at a set time in the hotel lobby, drive him to his meetings, and staff his book table. I learned from Pastor Bill how to be the voice for the children who couldn't speak up for themselves. I learned how to share God's heart for a young generation every time I had access to the churches or ministries that invited me. Pastor Bill taught me how to create a team of partners and the importance of consistent, compelling communication. While I traveled, we lived in the basement. I would leave on Saturday or Sunday and return Monday or Tuesday. I traveled almost every week while Tricia, Cheryl, and Juanita carried the ministry load. These women were supported by the Teen Leaders who took care of the details of set up and tear down of the church for services. Teens were eligible to join Teen Leadership at twelve years old, because twelve was a critical age of decision for our kids who started attending Sidewalk Sunday School when they were only three or four. Twelve is the age when a child chooses to embrace the gangster, or street, lifestyle or solidify their commitment to God.

We wanted Teen Leadership to be a coveted position that younger kids could look up to and follow. As the Teen Leaders gained authority and experience in ministry to their neighborhood peers, every child in Sidewalk Sunday School aspired to be in Teen Leadership. We raised money through child sponsorship to allow Teen Leaders to attend an overnight retreat in Lake Geneva, Wisconsin, for leadership training; wear a special Teen Leadership T-shirt; and help lead and serve in the ministry. Our goal was for each teen leader to grow into a stable, mature adult that was a pillar of the church.

My vision for what the teens would become was as real to me as the challenges we were currently facing. In faith, I wrote on the whiteboard in our basement apartment that my goal was to one day, have thirty staff members and a million dollar budget. I set this goal even though it looked impossible since we were eating out of the food pantry, living in the basement, and driving the church van. We still didn't own any vehicles and every dime that came in from the fund raising ministry trips went towards programs for the kids. The travel schedule was grueling, but I knew I had to tell the story of what God was doing with our ministry as we reached kids from the southern portion of Wisconsin to the northern shore of Illinois. The nation needed to know that a generation was being reached for God.

Sierra was one of those kids. She started attending Church of Joy at twelve years old. She didn't know at the time that she was coming to meet God. She and her friend were coming to church to meet boys at a Christian hip-hop concert that we were hosting for our youth group. That night, after the concert ended, I spent the rest of the service helping the teens to understand that they weren't on the earth by mistake. God has a unique and personal plan for each of our lives, and we have to seek God to find that purpose. Even though I didn't know it at the time, the message hit God's target in Sierra's life. She was now looking for more than boys; she came back to church

looking for a relationship with God. Sierra eventually became a teen leader who helped in classes, answered phones, and helped set up for services. As Sierra became more involved, we learned that she loved to dance and sing. In her mind, her future was to become one of the girls that she saw in music videos, but that wasn't God's plan. God wanted to use her gifts of creativity, dance, and song to be a blessing in His house. As she grew in her relationship with Christ, she learned to seek God as her one and only passion. She is now our praise and worship leader.

God wasn't only using Sidewalk Sunday School in the lives of little girls. Demitrius was a three-year-old little boy when he came to a Sidewalk Sunday School outreach in the early days when we met in King Park. Demitrius was stout with a quick laugh and wide smile; he was the youngest of six kids. His older brothers and sisters eventually got involved with local gangs. Some nights after church, Demitrius went home to drug deals taking place in his living room and random shootings aimed at his apartment.

The lives of our children were fragile because of their environment, which threatened to crush their indomitable spirit. The early days of Sidewalk allowed me to meet so many of God's wonderful children. Thin, with studious brown eyes and a bright complexion, Shakrisha was the daughter of my sister's best friend from high school.

Shakrisha came to the first Sidewalk Sunday School service in Cole Park at four years old when she was living in the projects in North Chicago. Because of Sidewalk Sunday School, she gained an opportunity to hear God's Word as she sat in the field with the other children. She became a Christian at eight years old, standing behind a Sidewalk Sunday School truck, when I led the kids in a prayer for salvation. Although she had a bright spirit, there was always a sadness in her big, brown eyes. I didn't know then about the constant drama and abuse she suffered. She had seen too much in her young years, and she had to work really hard not to be overwhelmed with how she felt inside. I encouraged her and did what I could for her each time I came to the neighborhood to pick up children for church. She was always eager to participate and looked at Sidewalk Sunday School as a way to find light in her family darkness. I found out years later that her mother was sexually abused as a teenager by her father. Her mother's traumatic experience of constant abuse gave me a clue as to her mother's pattern of being with abusive men, men who unleashed a wave of violence that swept up even the smallest members of the family. Her mother would find freedom in Christ years later and be set free from her dark past while finding a new way of life.

The children of Sidewalk Sunday School had stories that were strangely similar, although the way that the ministry impacted these children was unique. When I think about a child like Kiki Lee, I'm reminded of God's sovereignty—His ability to see ahead and provide so far beyond anything that we know to ask for. For Kiki, she had a challenging family life, as one of seven kids in her family. Her mom was involved in drugs and prone to hanging out with violent people. Kiki always asked the Sidewalk Sunday School bus driver to drop her off last because she dreaded walking into an apartment with fighting and chaos. Her older brothers and sisters initially attended church with her, but they eventually drifted away as time and opportunity allowed them to escape their violent home.

Kiki started coming to Sidewalk Sunday Services at four years old. When she turned twelve, she joined the Teen Leadership team and I noticed her gift of serving. I knew she was trying as hard as she could to be at the services, despite her mom's tumultuous lifestyle marked by drugs and violence. With her upbeat, happy demeanor, you would have no idea that she was dealing with constant fighting at home.

Kiki's mom finally hit rock bottom and started living in a van while trying to figure out how to keep her kids fed. She realized that she couldn't live the life she wanted with the responsibility of her kids. She dropped Kiki off in front of a friend's job and told Kiki to go live with her. When I saw Kiki again, I was reminded that we needed a home for girls who wanted to follow God but had no place to live. I knew we could make a difference and one day we would. We bought a girls' home a year later, and we now have a boys' home for young people when they turn eighteen and have nowhere to go.

Kiki's crisis wasn't unique, but it was different from the daily challenge faced by Shakrisha. Shakrisha always made sure that I knew that she was there. For her, it was a miracle to have a man take interest in her, especially one who made sure that she had fun, was safe, and experienced a time of joy— even though there wasn't a lot to be happy about in her life.

I knew that if Church of Joy and Sidewalk Sunday School didn't exist, Sierra, Kiki, Demitrius and Shakrisha would become another statistic. They would become another drug addict, gang member, single mom, or irresponsible teenage father who didn't take care of his children. Church of Joy and Sidewalk Sunday School was their ticket out of a lifestyle of generational poverty, drug addiction, fatherlessness, and abuse. Demitrius, Kiki, Shakrisha, and so many children like them, hugged me every time they saw me after I returned from my fundraising ministry trips. Their laughter, smiles, and hugs reminded me that I was their voice. I was their voice to a group of people in most churches that would never know they existed in a war zone in our own backyards. I knew that God sent me to them and to the churches of America to show the church the desperate circumstances that millions of children were living in right under their noses. I gave Christians an opportunity to respond to the need.

Chapter 27

MORE THAN A MINISTRY

*Learn to do right; seek justice. Defend the oppressed. Take
up the cause of the fatherless; plead the case of the widow.*
—Isaiah 1:17

THE ONLY WAY to truly impact and change lives with the Gospel is by building relationships. This is what our ministry has been built on—relationships with these young people, and helping them in every aspect of their lives.

Our Teen Leadership program became a turning point for the teenagers. We didn't realize how much of an impact this program would have. This program helps teenagers through accountability, mentorship, and character development, and it gives the teens an opportunity to learn, develop, and use their gifts and talents in the ministry. It is a phenomenal program for teenagers.

When we accepted new applications from the kids for Teen Leadership, Shakrisha couldn't wait. Although she was only eleven, and the required age was twelve, she lied just so that she could be a part of it all and be more involved at the church. When I found out that Shakrisha lied about her age, I was disappointed because everyone understood that being on Teen Leadership was a privilege. On the Sunday of the next Teen Leadership meeting, I remember asking her about her dishonesty. She looked down and began to cry and said, "I just wanted to help you, Pastor Louie." Her heart to serve moved me, and I asked her to promise me that she would never quit. "I won't, Pastor Louie," she said. "I won't ever quit Teen Leadership."

We began to notice that as these teenagers were now at the church more often for this program, a lot of them were struggling in school. Part of the requirement for Teen Leadership was for the teen leaders to show us their report card and get reports from teachers on their behavior. We had to hold them accountable so they could be leaders.

As we began to keep these young people accountable, I started to get reports on kids like Shakrisha and Demetrius; they were not doing well and were even being disrespectful at school. I found myself having to go up to the schools to help these kids. The schools began to learn of my involvement in these kids' lives; they understood that I was there to help these young people. One afternoon, the guidance counselor called me because Shakrisha's mom didn't have a phone, and she didn't have a way to contact her about Shakrisha's hostility towards the teachers and staff. After the call, I put the phone down, got in the church van, and drove to the school. The counselor was surprised to see me so quickly, but when I knew that something needed to be done, I did it quickly. I learned that from Bill Wilson, Pastor Mark at Grace Fellowship, and the military. A priority problem demanded a priority response. Shakrisha would know that her attitude and schoolwork were a priority by my response.

Shakrisha was surprised and shaken to see me sitting in the counselor's office. "Pastor Louie!" She exclaimed as she walked in and sat down.

"Shakrisha, why are you acting up?" I asked. I also learned to be a straight shooter when you're dealing with problems.

She looked down at her shoes and then said matter-of-factly, "Because I'm mad."

"Why are you mad, Shakrisha?"

"Because I feel stupid," she said softly. "I don't understand any of the work. The other kids call me dumb."

I knew the humiliation and helplessness of not understanding basic math or English. I knew from sitting in a cube isolated from the rest of my friends how feeling stupid can make you angry. I decided that I would give Shakrisha what I never received sitting in a cubical so many years ago in an elementary school that left me alone to teach myself.

As I returned to the church, I knew what I needed to do. That afternoon, Tricia and I set up a tutoring area at the church for Shakrisha and other kids who were struggling. Every day they came directly from school to the church to receive tutoring in remedial reading and math; they were pushed, pressed, and encouraged to learn. What happened next was amazing.

I continually saw that kids like Shakrisha and Demetrius were smart, they just had so many negative things going on at home that it hindered them from learning and focusing in school. My daughter Madison was going to Christian school at that time; she was about seven years old, and I really liked the school. I began to think about the possibility of getting Shakrisha and Demetrius sponsored to attend as well. I sat with both of them and told them, "I believe in you, you are smarter than you think and God has a great plan for your life. I am considering enrolling you into the Christian School that Madison attends." They had smiles from ear to ear. However, I told them, "I will not enroll you if you keep acting up the rest of the school year, and I will look at your grades before we make any decision." The school ended after several months, and it was time to see where they were. I was in awe when I found out Shakrisha did not get into trouble at all, and her grades had gotten better. Then Demetrius came back with his report card; his grades were better too, and he made it on the honor roll! Shakrisha and Demetrius graduated from the Christian School, both on the honor roll! Praise the Lord!

I learned a lot through working with these two young people. If you give a young person vision and encouragement and hold them accountable, they will succeed.

Sidewalk Sunday School was going to be more than just a church for children and teens. We were going to respond to the needs of our children. Even though Tricia and I were still living in the basement of the church, we were going to find a way to feed the hungry, clothe the naked, and educate those who were falling through the cracks of the educational system.

Chapter 28

FROM SACRIFICE TO BLESSING

And if anyone gives even a cup of cold water to one
of these little ones who is my disciple, truly I tell you,
that person will certainly not lose their reward.
—MATTHEW 10:42

ALTHOUGH WE WERE making a great impact, we were still challenged financially. Tricia and I were sitting downstairs in the basement, and all of a sudden, all the electricity went out. The basement was pitch black. In the darkness, I asked Tricia, "Did we pay the electric bill?" All Tricia could say was, "No, we don't have any money to pay it." Tricia called the electric company the next day and pleaded with them to turn the lights on and set us up on a payment plan. The lady told Tricia, "Most people go to their church for assistance in situations like this."

Tricia responded, "We are a church," then wrapped up the call.

Even our bank was done with us. I tried to juggle the needs and the finances that were coming in; at times, we had to float checks in hope that I would raise the support at a church or someone would mail in a donation. The bank officer over our account called us in to meet with him at the bank. We had an idea of why he wanted to meet us. Our bank account was overdrawn, and they were ready to close out our account. Right before we got to the bank, I felt the Holy Spirit tell me to check our post office box. Tricia kept telling me, "We are already late; we just need to go to the bank." I decided to go to the post office. There was one envelope. I opened it to find a note that said, "I thought you might need this!" Enclosed was a check for $11,000, enough to cover our account and cover some bills. Praise God, we handed the bank officer the check and our account remained open.

After many years of sacrifices and challenges to keep our ministry afloat, we began to see little trickles of God's blessing and hand over our ministry and us. We were leasing our church building and the owners were getting frustrated that we kept getting behind in our rent. One afternoon Tricia and I were in our church van getting ready to go somewhere when the owner of our building pulled up swiftly to our truck. We knew why he was there; we were six months behind in rent, which added up to $24,000. There was no way to pay him at that moment, and I was aware he could evict us.

Ken, the owner, looked at me with frustration and demanded we give him the rent money for all six months. I looked at him, eye to eye, and said, "Ken, I know we are behind, and we are trying to do everything we can to get you your money." At that moment, he turned to his wife sitting in the passenger seat then turned back to me with a different countenance and said, "Louie, here's what I am going to do; don't worry about the $24,000, and from now I will cut your rent in half, which is $2,000; get it to me on time." I told him OK and thank you, then he just drove off. Tricia and I sat in the truck for a moment astonished that God would turn the heart of that man to give us grace and allow us to stay in our building with a discounted rent amount. We were overwhelmed as we started to see the Lord watching over us.

> Tricia and I were so overwhelmed; it was as if our heavenly Father said, "I have seen your sacrifice and obedience to what I've called you to do. I will now open up My checkbook in heaven. What do you need?"

We were so grateful to the Lord every time we saw His blessings trickle down. We were continuing to reach the children, and it just kept growing. One day I looked outside and saw developers looking at our property and the properties around us. I knew change was coming, but I didn't know how or when. My relationship with the owner of our building was shaky, and I thought *what if one of these developers offers him a large amount of money to buy this property, and he sells it from underneath us*? I put together a proposal to put before some of my top donors asking them to help us with the down payment. I told them that we needed to purchase this property; I felt our landlord would be ready to get it off their hands. We waited a few days after giving the proposal to the donors, but they didn't just help with the down payment, they gave our ministry the largest donation we had ever received. When we sat down, they looked over at us and said they wanted to help; they purchased our church building for us.

I could see now that God was setting all of this up. These generous partners really began to invest in the lives of the children. They took an interest and began asking if we had other needs. I shared with them that we had approximately $170,000 of debt; they wrote the check, and it was paid off. They saw I needed more buses and vans to pick up more children; they wrote the check, and we had more vehicles for the children. They also purchased a piece of property to park all of our vehicles. Tricia and I were so overwhelmed; it was as if our heavenly Father said, "I have seen your sacrifice and obedience to what I've called you to do. I will now open up My checkbook in heaven. What do you need?"

Reflecting on all that God was doing to advance us, provide for us, and help us make more of an impact, we were still living in the basement. I began to see that the ministry was growing and gaining more influence in the lives of these young people. I felt encouraged. One day my wife and I were sitting downstairs in the basement. I looked at her and said, "Trish, I know it's been tough going through everything and living here in the basement. I don't see ourselves moving out any time soon. God has been providing so much for us; we just need to be thankful. Here's what I want you to do; go buy some pictures for the walls and decorate our little apartment so it feels more like home." Although it was hard to say, I felt a peace within me. We had been living there for about three years, and I figured we'd possibly be there for another five to ten.

I settled it in my heart, "I'm not quitting; I'm not stopping, and God will help us. He wants a generation reached." My wife and I kept ministering to the children; we both drove our bus routes every week picking up children, and I continued to travel to raise financial support. Through my travels, I met so many wonderful and generous donors. I met one particular businessman who came to visit our ministry. After the visit, we took him downstairs to our area to share more of what we do. At that time, we did not want people to know we were living there. We didn't know how people would respond knowing we lived in the basement of the church.

This potential donor looked at us and asked us directly, "Are you and your family living here in the basement?"

My stomach dropped. I thought to myself, *someone from the outside is going to know we live here. What is he going to think?*" I dropped my head and told the gentleman, "Yes we do." I began to tell him what had happened— how we lost our home and how our vehicles were repossessed. I explained to him that when we began reaching so many children and started bringing them to church, our church congregation left. At that moment, he looked at me and said, "You are doing so much for these children, and the impact you are making is incredible. You and your family cannot keep living here trying to do what you are doing. Here's what I want you and Tricia to do; look for a house that will best suit you and your family and bring the information to my office by next week." Tricia and I sat on our bed that night and wept; we couldn't believe the Lord was looking out for us. He didn't leave us, and He wanted to bless us personally for our obedience and sacrifice.

This gentleman didn't just buy us a house, he insisted that we build it from scratch and get the kind of house we wanted. When we closed on the house, we looked across the table at him and said, "Thank you!"

With a tear in his eye he said, "No, thank you. You don't see Christians like you sacrifice for the kind of children you reach."

The Bible says in Matthew 19:29, "And everyone who has left houses or brothers or sisters or father or mother or wife or children or fields for my sake will receive a hundred times as much and will inherit eternal life." We saw this scripture played out in our lives. We lost a house for His name's sake, and He blessed us with a brand-new house.

At that time, Madison was seven years old, and we were so thankful that we could have better living conditions for her, including a backyard where she could play. Life was getting more stable for us, and we felt we could breathe a little better. Tricia and I had been working closely with Shakrisha, who was thirteen years old and a teen leader. We knew her mom really well, and her mom shared with us she couldn't raise Shakrisha. She was worn out from her older kids. We were close to Shakrisha, and we knew that she couldn't be tossed around from home to home. We decided to take Shakrisha into our home. We enrolled Shakrisha into the Christian school Madison was attending. Living with us was a difficult adjustment for her; she wasn't used to the order, accountability, and father figure that would talk to her. It is not easy raising other people's children. She remained with us until she graduated high school. A year after she moved in with us, a teenager that grew up in our ministry had a baby at seventeen years old. This teen mom was close to Tricia and me, and we did everything we could to help and support her. When her son, Travion, was about two years old, this teen mom was struggling to care for him. There was a possibility that DCFS was going to be called on her, so we stepped in and took Travion into our home as well. Travion lived with us for two years until his mom was stable to take him back.

From time to time, youth groups from around the nation would visit as a missionary trip to help us. Aureal was a teenager that came with one particular youth group from Colorado. She was so captured by our ministry that she told us when she graduated, she was coming back to help us and be a part of our ministry. She did exactly what she said and moved out to where we were. At that time, we had Shakrisha and Travion living with us, and we opened our home to Aureal as well. We had quite the Brady Bunch.

Travion was three, Madison was seven, Shakrisha was fifteen, and Aureal was eighteen. In a two-year span, we went from one child to four. Tricia and I always said wanted a big family, at least four children. We learned so much during this season, and we knew the Lord had given us this house to take in these children.

After a few years, Travion went back to live with his mom, Shakrisha graduated high school and went off to college, and we continued to raise Madison. We had Madison very young, when we first started the ministry; we put having more children on hold because of all that we were going through with building the ministry and the stress it brought with it. Tricia looked at me one day and said, "Louie, if we are going to have more children, we better try soon. We are getting older, and Madison is almost ten years old." I agreed and we were excited to have more children. Within a year of that conversation, Tricia got pregnant. We were so happy; we told our church and called our friends and family. Our life was finally settling down, and we were able to start doing things we couldn't do before. I knew Tricia was so happy to have another child. I went with her to the appointment where we were going to hear the heartbeat. It was such a special moment for us; finally we were having more children! *2 miscarriages*

As the nurse looked for the heartbeat, she looked concerned. We waited, and finally she looked up at us and told us she couldn't find the heartbeat. I saw Tricia's countenance change, and I didn't know what to think. They ran some tests; we had lost our baby. We were devastated; however, I tried to be strong for Tricia and reminded her that we had Madison and that we could try again. We waited about six months before trying again. Once more, Tricia got pregnant. This time we didn't tell anyone until Tricia went to the doctor and all was well with our second baby. Tricia went to her appointment to hear the heartbeat; for some reason I was not able to go this time. Tricia called me right after her appointment crying—we had lost our baby again.

It was bitter sweet for Tricia; she would see a teen girl that we were ministering to with a baby and think *why can't I have another baby?* We both felt disappointed and hurt; we waited almost ten years to add to our family. We didn't understand how we could reach thousands of other people's children while we were struggling to have more children of our own. It took some time, for as they say, "time heals." Tricia and I talked about our options for adding to our family. I told Tricia that we should consider adoption. Tricia is adopted, so I knew that it was dear to her heart. As we continued to pray and think about our options, we found out Tricia was pregnant again. We didn't know what to think; we just prayed and rejoiced in the Lord.

The two miscarriages took a toll on Tricia; however, this time when she went to the doctor, there was a heartbeat, and months later we found out it was a boy. Matthew Luis Reyes was born in 2008.

We named him Matthew because he is a gift from God. The Lord didn't just give us a child, He gave me a boy to carry on my name. We are so grateful to have two amazing children, Madison and Matthew.

Chapter 29

RAISING UP THE YOUNGER GENERATION

And they that shall be of thee shall build the old waste
places: thou shalt raise up the foundations of many
generations; and thou shalt be called, The repairer of
the breach, The restorer of paths to dwell in.

—Isaiah 58:12, kjv

GOD SHOWED ME why He was opening the windows of heaven over our ministry. "The King will reply, 'Truly I tell you, whatever you did for one of the least of these brothers and sisters of mine, you did for me'" (Matthew 25:40).

For many years, we were reaching the least, ministering to the children from the streets, feeding them, helping them with school, and loving them unconditionally. When we were bringing children to church, Jesus was coming in the door with them. God says in His word, "That entire generation passed away, and after them grew up a generation who did not know the Lord or the deeds that He had done for Israel" (Judges 2:10, mev). God wants the younger generation to know Him, to make Him Lord over their lives, and to serve Him.

With all that the Lord was providing, I felt the urgency to do more to help these children. Our generous donors helped us lease and renovate an 8,000 square foot facility for our Success Center.

The Success Center is a place where children who are struggling in their academics can come after school, in our vans, and get help. The Success Center is empowering the next generation in academics. So many of these children struggle in academics due to the emotional chaos at home—neglect, abuse, fatherlessness—and some have learning disabilities and behavioral disorders. The Student Achievement program provides remedial training, tutoring, afterschool homework help, and enrichment activities. These programs reduce the achievement gap and give the children confidence and skills needed for school. Our academic program became very successful. Children would come into the program reading two to three grades below their grade level. After completing a year in the program, they made great progress. Many of these children would end the year reading at or above their grade level. I know I would have done better in school and not had to sit in a wooden cube if the Success Center had been made available to me in elementary school.

I believe the greatest thing that can change the destiny of a child is a personal relationship with Jesus, and the second thing is empowering them academically and giving them vision for their lives. From the beginning of my ministry, I have always told children and teenagers, "God has a plan for your life." To this day, young people come up and tell me that I impacted their lives by telling them this: "God has a plan for your life." The younger generation needs Jesus, purpose, vision, and mentorship to succeed. They want God, and they want to be mentored and kept accountable.

As we ministered through the years, we began to see the young people growing up. People would ask me, "Are these young people growing up and going to college to become lawyers or doctors?"

I would simply say, "I know what they are not going to be—drug dealers, gang members, drug addicts, teen mothers, and so on."

This was reality for these young people; they just needed to break the cycles in their families so they could be free and live a different lifestyle. As many of these young people were getting ready to graduate, I realized I had to do something to further help them. Many of them would tell me that they wanted to help in the ministry and work at the church after graduation. I also knew for some that they would not make it at college. I helped some of the young people enlist in the military. The United States Army changed my life; I gave these young people that option. For some of the young people, I knew they needed to help me reach the younger generation just as I reached them.

I felt it would be good to send some of these young people, those who wanted to stay and work in the ministry, to Bible College. I was able to get donors to sponsor several of these young people to go to a well-known Bible college in Columbus, Ohio.

I was so proud to see two of them graduate; the others were still taking classes. One day God spoke to me. He showed me that I was a voice to this younger generation; I was a spiritual father to these young people. God told me, "You have to raise them up." Then the big word came: "Start your own Bible college for these young people; they want to be here and help you. Train them up." This all came to me during a Friday evening service. Immediately after the service was over, I put a call into the students. As they all stood around one of their phones I shared with them what God spoke to me, and I ended with, "I'm bringing you home." Every one of them agreed and were so excited to be a part of pioneering our Bible college.

After processing what God said, I sat up that night and thought, "How do I start a Bible college?" I didn't know where to start. I am so grateful to the Lord, He brought some amazing staff to help me during that time, and we put our heads together, researched, and prayed. We brought the young people home after that school year in May and started our new Bible college in August.

I leased out a small building that was across from our church for the college; it was perfect. I purchased T-shirts for the students that had our Bible college name and logo. The first day, we walked across the street to our new college with our T-shirts on and took a picture in front of the building. What a moment; I knew then we were making history. I knew we were laying a foundation for many generations. For most of these young people, they are the first in their families to go to college.

Of course, any time you start something new you have to work out the kinks. Just as if I had sent my own daughter to college, I realized I had to treat them as my own children. I had to provide housing, food, transportation, and free tuition. I continued to raise financial support to make sure these young people could go to our Bible college.

We own two homes, one for the young ladies and one for the young men. We also use these homes for young people that are not enrolled in our college if they are in a crisis.

We lease five apartments, as well, for these young people. As the Bible college started, we created an internship program for these students to help in the day-to-day operations and receive hands-on training in ministry. They work in areas such as children's and youth ministry, they drive buses and vans to pick up the children, they lead our Sidewalk Sunday School outreach trucks, and minister to children that live in their old neighborhoods. They work in graphic design and media, music ministry, and administration. Tricia and I love watching these young people grow up and discover their gifts and talents; we love watching them fulfill God's purpose in their lives. Our Bible college is a four-year school, and it has changed our whole ministry. Many of these young people will graduate and work on staff. The ministry continued to grow and we needed more room.

Chapter 30

GOD WANTS TO BE GLORIFIED

*Then He who sat on the throne said, "Behold, I
make all things new." And He said to me, "Write,
for these words are true and faithful."*
—Revelation 21:5, nkjv

OUR MINISTRY HAD gotten to the point where we needed more
room to grow. We now had a thriving adult congregation that
loved the children. I knew that our little warehouse church in
Zion, Illinois, that housed the ministry for thousands of children could not
accommodate the wonderful families and adults that began to attend. I knew
we had to find something bigger, but the question was where and when? I
began looking for land; I found some great pieces of land on the outskirts of
Zion. I envisioned a beautiful brand new church building sitting on ten to
fifteen acres. I began to share the vision with some of our donors, and they
wanted to help.

As I was daily looking for property, I received a phone call. One of our
donors called me to let me know that the YMCA building in Waukegan was
for sale. I wasn't too thrilled with that idea. Honestly, I didn't want to put
my church in Waukegan; that's where I grew up, and I would be reminded of
the difficult memories. I knew many people were moving out of Waukegan.

I wasn't comfortable with making this kind of move or with the possibility of hurting our church. My wife and I went into a meeting with the donors that called me about the property. I remember coaching Tricia before we went in; I told her, "Whatever you do, don't let them convince us to take this property; we have to build on the outskirts of Zion like we envisioned." I had a plan; Tricia and I were ready.

As soon as they began to talk about the property, I felt the Lord tell me to humble myself and not to say anything. After I left that meeting, I went home and cried a little. I didn't know why God wanted us to move to Waukegan. I called my pastor, Dr. Mark Cowart in Colorado, and I shared what was going on and how I was feeling. He said one thing to me that caught my attention. He said, "Brother Louie, unless Jesus comes down from heaven and tells you no, you need to consider it. If you try to build brand new, it could set your ministry back ten to fifteen years."

I was in my study one evening, and the Lord brought to my attention a dream I wrote down a few years back. I'm not one to dream much; however, for some reason, I wrote it down. I pulled it out, and this is what I had written: "I decided to move my church to Waukegan. I went to the mayor's office, who was my driver's ed teacher in high school, and told him I was considering moving my ministry to Waukegan. He looked at me and said, "Welcome home; we want you here."

I asked him "What about the permits to renovate?"

He replied, "Don't worry, Louie, it's done." I couldn't believe I had that dream a few years before this. I felt it was confirmation, and I needed to trust God.

I now had a peace about moving to Waukegan; it's about six miles from our Zion location. We went back to our donors and told them we were ready to do this, and they were glad they found us a facility to house our entire ministry headquarters. I found it interesting that we were going to move our ministry to an old YMCA facility. I can remember when I was twelve years old, my friends invited me to the Y to play basketball. When we got there and went inside, my two friends had their membership ID, showed it, and went right in. I was left at the door because I did not have a membership or four dollars to get in. I was poor, and I didn't have anything. That was the last time I was in that facility. Now here I was, about to own it—God is good.

As we continued to collaborate with our donors about the plan, they made it clear they were not going to do much renovation because of the cost. Again, the Lord told me to humble myself and be thankful for whatever they did.

There were thirteen organizations looking at the property; to my surprise, our donor was ready to pay cash. That definitely put us in the front of the line and we purchase the 55,000 square foot property. We began working with architects on the renovation of the facility. I was concerned about the city approving the permits, and then an interesting thing happened; the current mayor told us, "Don't worry! It's done, whatever you need." As we kept working, we found out that our donors had approved for the entire inside of the facility to be renovated. It took a year before it was all complete and ready for us to move in. The purchase and renovation was a multi-million dollar project. Again, the Lord was setting us up to expand and grow.

The facility turned out beautifully, and it looked nothing like the YMCA. Our 55,000 square foot facility has a main sanctuary, a youth sanctuary, seven classrooms, a café, a commercial grade kitchen, offices, a gym, a recording studio, and dance studio. Most of the rooms in this facility are designated for the younger generation.

This was a financial miracle! Churches don't always get millions of dollars donated at one time. This happened because we've put a priority on the younger generation. God wants a generation reached. I have seen God do miracle after miracle for this younger generation.

What I did find out after putting our church in Waukegan was that the people wanted it. We had our ribbon cutting ceremony, and the mayor was right there with us as we both cut the ribbon. Then we had our grand opening, and so many people came out for that.

The first year we moved in, we began to fill up with people that loved our ministry and wanted to get involved. After the first year, we immediately went to two services. The people in Waukegan and the surrounding cities wanted a church just like ours, one that was putting a priority on the younger generation.

As Tricia and I reflected through this process, we were very grateful to the Lord, and we knew we had paid a great price to be where we were at. Our word for the year was, "All things new." We knew we were in a new season and a new beginning for Church of Joy, Reach A Generation.

Chapter 31

A VOICE TO THE NATION

No matter our childhood, our jobs, or our beliefs, we all have one thing in common: Legacy. We see in God's Word how you can pass down generational blessings or curses. Someone must rise up within a family or a church and be a voice for righteousness to be carried on from generation to generation. Life is too short to waste time and not leaving a spiritual legacy a priority.

I HAVE MINISTERED TO children and teenagers for over twenty years. I felt an unction from the Holy Spirit a year before we moved that my season of ministering to the children was coming to an end. I had mixed emotions about that. I have a strong anointing over my life to minister to children and teenagers. Prior to the Holy Spirit speaking to me, I had begun training my sixteen-year-old daughter, Madison, to teach the children. As soon as she went on that stage, I knew she had it. The Lord has passed my anointing to minister to young people to Madison.

As we got closer to moving, I let Madison have the whole service so she could learn how to run an entire service. There was normally about 500 children every week. The children really loved Madison, and they wanted to hear what she had to say.

A month before we moved, we put together a legacy event for our church. This is where I was going to officially appoint Madison as my replacement and pastor over the children. The church gathered around Madison, and everyone supported her in this new role. Four years prior to this, I created a kids TV show for children in Chicago to watch. We broadcasted our services for the children. I felt I needed to give Madison an opportunity to host the show. I noticed one time when we were praying that Madison had a unique voice, and it would go well on TV.

After the first season, we changed the show up a little and named it "Maddie Rey." It became a reality TV show about a Christian teenager, and it was filled with Christian music and dancing.

As we watched her bloom in front of the camera, we began to notice how well she sang. She began writing and producing music CD's. I looked at Maddie and saw the strong anointing she has to minister to children as well as the anointed, beautiful singing voice she has. She's a lot like me, very bold, and she lives out loud for Jesus.

I felt God was showing me how to take our ministry to another level. He was showing me that I needed to just pastor the adult congregation, coach, and continue to train the staff and our interns; I would continue to be a voice for this younger generation. I was encouraged as I saw how the Lord kept showing me how to set up the ministry through the years. For instance, starting the Bible college when we did was God's timing. The first students graduated the year we moved into our new facility. After graduating, they began working on staff to help us with our growing ministry. It has also given them more ministry opportunities. I believe the next revival will come through a younger generation, and I am preparing my young people to be bold and ready to go after it!

Through the years, I began to sense that I had an apostolic anointing. God was using me to build ministries, bring spiritual order and honor back to the Lord in our region, and break the spiritual bondages over God's people through bold and prophetic teaching of God's Word. God has given me authority within my church and our region, and now He is opening doors on a national level. Our story has been featured in *Charisma* magazine, *Ministry Today*, and the *700 Club*. I know that God wants the younger generation reached, and He is using our story to encourage the body to have faith; it can be done.

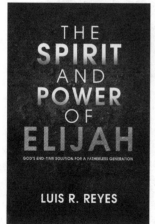

I have had the opportunity of sharing my story of faith to churches across the nation; I've also had the opportunity to train pastors and youth leaders on how to reach the younger generation. People from all over the nation visit our ministry to build their faith. The Lord gave me a book to write called, *The Spirit and Power of Elijah*. I wrote this book in thirty days; I knew the Lord wanted this message out to the body of Christ. The biggest epidemic in the world is fatherlessness. I wrote this book because of the tears of countless children that go to bed each night without a father, the weariness of many mothers, and the brokenness in many communities. God's solution for a fatherless generation is to raise up men who will take their place as fathers—to give their children an identity, to provide for their families, to strengthen their communities, and to reflect the compassion and strength of our heavenly Father.

I believe, as the scripture says in Malachi 4:5–6, "Behold, I will send you Elijah the prophet Before the coming of the great and dreadful day of the LORD. And he will turn The hearts of the fathers to the children, And the hearts of the children to their fathers, Lest I come and strike the earth with a curse" (NKJV). I am sharing this book with pastors, leaders, fathers, and the body to turn their hearts to the younger generation so their hearts can turn to the heavenly Father. God wants the younger generation to know Him. Elijah prepares a spiritual legacy for the up and coming generation through the authority of spiritual fathers in the house of God. God wants a joining of the generations. We must think generationally as the Jews did. So much was about the up and coming generation. All it takes is one lost generation to fall into paganism and atheism.

Elijah comes to make right what is wrong; the nation has gotten so far away from God. But God always swings a door of opportunity to bring change to a generation. Anytime that God wants to change a people, He doesn't start with those who are old, He goes to the younger generation, and He expects those who are older to raise that generation up in a better way and a better understanding from what we ever had.

When I came back to my hometown in 1997, I could have allowed myself to focus on all of the churches that had been established for decades, who were not pressing to reach the children in the streets.

I could have listened to the naysayers that said that it was impossible to build a church on children and teens. I could have given my attention to those who saw our efforts and mocked our Sidewalk trucks and who ridiculed us for losing everything and moving into the basement. Instead, I kept my eyes focused on seeing the vulnerability of our community and the spoils of reaching a generation for Christ. I had to be willing to walk the gutters in low-income housing. I had to be willing to knock on doors and deal with death threats as I infringed on the turf of the drug dealers who had turned local parks into drug distribution centers. I had to be willing to see the vulnerability of the neighborhoods I walked in, be willing to breathe in the stench of poverty, be willing to endure the agony of sending kids back into broken homes every week. I had to continue to sacrifice my life, and that of my family, to bring those children an hour or two of comfort every Saturday afternoon or on a Wednesday and Thursday night. Today, however, I have conquered like King David, and the voice of every accuser is silenced in the face of God's victory. To God be the glory; we praise Him, honor Him, and commit this younger generation to Him.

ABOUT THE AUTHOR

Growing up in an impoverished and rough neighborhood, Pastor Louis R. Reyes experienced the fear, insecurities, and neglect any child would growing up under these circumstances in this type of neighborhood. Because of the poverty and neglect he experienced at home, he was a very angry child and his resulting behavior caused him to spend twelve years in special education. Desperate to find a way out of the neighborhood, he found himself being exceptionally athletic and received a baseball scholarship to a local college. Unfortunately, due to the lack of family and financial support, he had to drop out and the only viable option was to enlist into the military.

He spent four and a half years in the United States Army where his leadership qualities really came to the surface, and he found himself moving up very quickly; he enjoyed serving his country. When he had settled on the idea that this would be his career, God came to him and began to call him to full-time ministry. At that time, he was serving in children's ministry at Church For All Nations in Colorado Springs, Colorado, under Dr. Mark Cowart. He became a children's pastor and really thrived in ministering to the children. Under his leadership there, volunteers tripled, and he grew the children's ministry very quickly.

As he was settling in there, he met his wife Tricia, who was also beginning to serve in children's ministry. Together they served, ministering to the children and settling into a good life there in Colorado Springs. But God had other plans. Because of his childhood, he never entertained the thought of moving back to where he grew up. Two years after Pastor Louie and Tricia got married, God spoke to him to move back to where he had grown up. As difficult as it was, he had to humble himself and trust God. It was then that God spoke to him and said, "There are children just like you that need to be reached." That settled it. With the blessing of their pastor, they loaded up a U-Haul truck and moved to Illinois to answer the call.

Their very first church service was on Sunday, February 23, 1997, and twenty-two people attended. They had no idea what would be required of them from that fateful day on. Through great sacrifice and loss, an impactful ministry to children was birthed. On Saturday, July 12, 1997, the outreach Sidewalk Sunday School was pioneered in Waukegan, Illinois, on the South Side in Pastor Louie's old neighborhood, which was filled with poverty, violence, drugs, and gangs.

Although they started the ministry with adults, as the mandate to reach children grew stronger, they experienced some very challenging times building the ministry. They lost their home to foreclosure and vehicles to repossession. It was at that time God was refining Pastor Louie for what was to come next. God supernaturally turned the ministry around and brought supernatural provision. His vision became clear to Pastor Louie, that God had called him to bring a message of revival, turning the hearts of the people back towards God. Through a three-year season of revival, God began to reveal to Pastor Louie the answer to the questions of why violence, poverty, premature death, and desolation ruled the streets of the inner city and affected the lives of so many of our youth. Fatherlessness is at the root, and the revelation came forth on the spirit of Elijah. Pastor Louie has now become a voice to men across the nation, proclaiming the message of Malachi 4:5–6, which declares that through the spirit of Elijah, God will turn the hearts of the fathers back to the children, and the hearts of children back to their fathers.

Today, Pastor Louie and his wife Tricia continue to pastor a thriving church congregation at The New Church of Joy in Waukegan, Illinois. He founded, and is the chancellor of, their School of Ministry Bible College and has opened the Success Center, which is an academic tutoring program for elementary children. He continues to make a great impact in the lives of children and teenagers. He travels across the nation bringing this message of hope in the *Spirit of Elijah*, which is empowering men to reach the younger generation, to turn their hearts back to their children, and to take their place as men of God. Pastor Louie and Tricia have two amazing children, Madison and Matthew.

CONTACT THE AUTHOR

To contact Pastor Reyes or to learn more about this ministry, visit www.luisreyesministries.com, www.thenewchurchofjoy.com, and www. reachageneration.com.

MORE GREAT RESOURCES AND INFORMATION
AVAILABLE NOW!

Invite Pastor Luis Reyes to come to your church or organization to share this inspiring story to infuse the faith of your leaders, church congregation or organization. Pastor Louie is also available to speak at seminars or conferences to help churches reach the younger generation.

To book Pastor Luis Reyes or for more resources please visit www.luisreyesministries.com
If you would like to plan a visit, feel free to email us at info@thenewchurchofjoy.com.

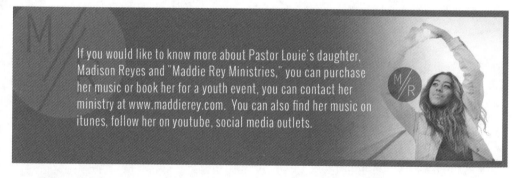

If you would like to know more about Pastor Louie's daughter, Madison Reyes and "Maddie Rey Ministries," you can purchase her music or book her for a youth event, you can contact her ministry at www.maddierey.com. You can also find her music on itunes, follow her on youtube, social media outlets.

Pastor Louie, his wife Tricia and their children are dedicated to reaching this younger generation and pray that through this book christians around the world will turn their hearts to the children so children's hearts will be turned to their Heavenly Father.

Visit us online for more products, resources and information.

 CHURCH OF JOY   LUISREYESMINISTRIES   REACH A GENERATION

 www.thenewchurchofjoy.com   www.luisreyesministries.com   www.reachageneration.com

❯ EFFECTIVELY IMPACTING
THE NEXT GENERATION

REACH THE YOUNG PEOPLE IN YOUR CHURCH AND YOUR COMMUNITY THE WAY GOD INTENDED YOU TO!

Pastor Luis R. Reyes
Founder & Senior Pastor
Church of Joy /
Reach A Generation

PASTOR LUIS R. REYES answered the call to reach young people in 1997 using a big yellow truck for mobile ministry outreach to 30 kids in a neighborhood park. In spite of adversity, discouragement and a lack of resources, Pastor Louie never abandoned his commitment to reach a generation for God!

❯ YEARS LATER, LOOK WHAT GOD CAN DO WHEN YOU STAY COMMITTED TO REACHING A GENERATION FOR HIM!

❯ FLEET OF BUSES, VANS & TRUCKS

❯ MULTIPLE OUTDOOR OUTREACH SITES

❯ AFTER SCHOOL TUTORING PROGRAM

❯ NUTRITIONAL PROGRAMS

❯ ANNUAL SUMMER CAMP AND OUTDOOR ACTIVITIES

❯ BOYS FOOTBALL PROGRAM

❯ BOYS BASKETBALL PROGRAM

❯ TEEN CREATIVE ARTS

❯ YOUTH OUTREACH & CONFERENCES

❯ STUDENT & INTERN HOUSING

❯ SCHOOL OF MINISTRY & BIBLE COLLEGE

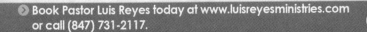

EVERYDAY A CHILD
DEPENDS ON US.

REACH A GENERATION

Make the choice today to
Support the life of a child!

- **Become a monthly partner** - $25, $50, $100 or more every month
- **Give a one-time gift** - $100, $500, $1000, $5000 or more
- **Contribute from your business or foundation** - (Any amount of your choice)
- **Leave a Legacy Gift** - Add Reach A Generation to your will, trust or estate plan.

WAYS TO GIVE:

- Give securely online at www.reachageneration.com
- Call in your credit or debit card contribution to (847) 731-2117. (You can also have your credit or debit card debited monthly for your partnership contribution.)
- Mail your check to Reach A Generation, P.O. Box 8397 Waukegan, IL 60079

Reach A Generation P.O. Box 8397 Waukegan, IL 60079 (847) 731-2117 info@thenewchurchofjoy.com www.reachageneration.com